Grammar Dimensions
Workbook Two

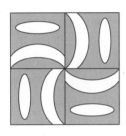

Cheryl Benz
*Miami-Dade Community
College*

Ann Roemer
*Miami-Dade Community
College*

Heinle & Heinle Publishers
A Division of Wadsworth, Inc.
Boston, Massachusetts 02116 U.S.A.

Photo Credits:
Photo on page 14 courtesy of Pat Martin.
Photo on page 54 courtesy of Red Cross.
Photo on page 119 courtesy of United Nations Library.
Photo on page 160 courtesy of Pat Martin.
Photo on page 178 courtesy of H. Armstrong Roberts.

Table of Contents

UNIT 1

Simple Present

Exercise 1 *(Focus 1)*

Read the following story about the students in a writing class. Underline the verbs which tell about habits (things they do again and again) or routines (things they do regularly) of the people in the class. Circle the verbs which tell about a lack of routine or habit. The first one has been done for you as an example.

Writing is my favorite class because of my classmates. Even though they work hard to improve their writing, they like to have fun too. Raul and Suzette study the hardest. They always listen carefully to the directions and raise their hands when they have a question. They are good students, and they try to help other students too. Jean Marc also participates in class. He is good at finding mistakes. Before I rewrite my papers, I always take them to him. There is only one student who doesn't participate in class—Yaniv. He always interrupts students, eats, and even sleeps in class. Besides that, he never pays attention. The only time he writes is when he passes notes to Su-Ling. He always teases her. Su-Ling is very shy and doesn't know how to act towards him.

Exercise 2 *(Focus 1)*

Write five sentences about the habits or routines of your classmates.

EXAMPLE: *Sandy always comes on time.*

1. _____

2. _____

3. _____

1

4. _____

5. _____

Exercise 3 (Focus 2)

The following are the responses of some of my classmates to a survey our teacher did.

Do you...	Yes	Sometimes	No
1. discuss politics with native English speakers?	Raul	Valentina Suzette	Yaniv
2. listen to the radio in English?	Valentina	Jean Marc	Wan-Yin
3. watch movies or TV in English?	Mohammed	Su-Ling	Yaniv
4. speak English at work or school?	Jean Marc Wan-Yin	Valentina	
5. read English language newspapers or magazines?	Suzette	Roberto Jean Marc	Yaniv Valentina
6. go to English class everyday?	Su-Ling Wan-Yin	Yaniv	
7. write letters in English?	Suzette Raul	Valentina	Su-Ling
8. practice English with native speakers?	Roberto	Yaniv	Valentina

Using the chart above, answer the following questions in complete sentences.

1. Who listens to the radio in English?

_____

2. Who writes letters in English?

_____

3. Who doesn't read English language newspapers or magazines?

_____

4. Who doesn't discuss politics with English speakers?

_____

5. Who doesn't watch movies in English?

_____

6. Who speaks English at work or school?

_____

7. Who goes to English class everday?

_____

8. Who practices with native speakers?

_____

9. Who watches movies or TV in English?

_____

10. Who doesn't listen to the radio in English?

_____

Give short answers for the following questions.

1. Does Roberto practice English with native speakers? _____

2. Do Suzette and Jean Marc read English language newspapers or magazines?

_____

3. Do Yaniv and Valentina read English language newspapers or magazines?

_____

4. Does Mohammed watch movies or TV in English? _____

5. Does Valentina practice English with native speakers? _____

Complete five questions about the chart.

1. Does _____ ?
2. Do _____ ?
3. Does _____ ?
4. Do _____ ?
5. Does _____ ?

Exercise 4 (Focus 3)

Survey

How often do you use the following strategies to practice English? Take the survey on the next page. Make a check (✔) in the box that applies to you.

How often do you ...	Always	Often	Sometimes	Rarely	Never
1. discuss politics with native English speakers?					
2. listen to the radio in English?					
3. watch movies or TV in English?					
4. speak English at work or school?					
5. read English language newspapers or magazines?					
6. go to English class?					
7. write letters in English?					
8. practice English with native speakers?					

Using the information above, write a complete sentence about how often you do each activity.

EXAMPLE: *I rarely discuss politics with English speakers.*

1. I _____ discuss politics with English speakers.
2. I _____ to the radio in English.
3. I _____
4. _____
5. _____
6. _____
7. _____
8. _____

Exercise 5 *(Focus 3)*   PAIR

Using the questions from Exercise 4, ask a classmate how often he or she does the activities. Write a complete sentence about how often he or she does each activity.

EXAMPLE: Q: *Abdul, how often do you discuss politics with native English speakers?*
                A: *I sometimes discuss politics with native English speakers.*
        You write: *Abdul sometimes discusses politics with native English speakers.*

1. _____
2. _____
3. _____

4. _____

5. _____

6. _____

7. _____

8. _____

Exercise 6 (*Focus 4*)

Make statements of fact by connecting the people in the first column with the appropriate action in the second column. Then write the sentence on the lines below using the correct form of the verb. The first one has been done for you as an example.

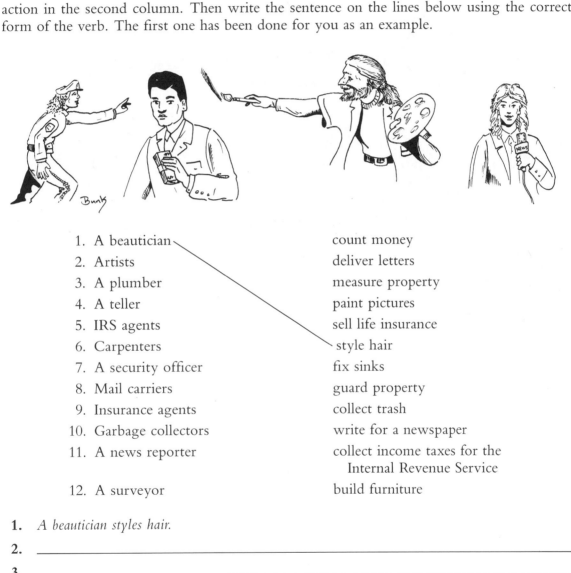

1. A beautician	count money
2. Artists	deliver letters
3. A plumber	measure property
4. A teller	paint pictures
5. IRS agents	sell life insurance
6. Carpenters	style hair
7. A security officer	fix sinks
8. Mail carriers	guard property
9. Insurance agents	collect trash
10. Garbage collectors	write for a newspaper
11. A news reporter	collect income taxes for the Internal Revenue Service
12. A surveyor	build furniture

1. *A beautician styles hair.*

2. _____

3. _____

4. _____

5. _____

6. _____

7. _____

8. _____

9. _____

10. _____

11. _____

12. _____

Exercise 7 (Focus 4)

Take turns with a partner asking questions about the jobs on the list. Give the short answer to the questions.

E X A M P L E :   A: *Does a security officer fix sinks?*
                   B: *No, she doesn't.*

                   B: *Do tellers count money?*
                   A: *Yes, they do.*

Present Progressive

Exercise 1 *(Focus 1)*

Read the following paragraph and underline both the **present progressive** verb forms and the **time expressions** that indicate that the actions are temporary or in progress. The first one has been done for you as an example.

Mohammed is an exchange student from Kuwait who's living in Toronto this academic year. His teachers and classmates are worried about him because he looks tired and is acting differently from the way he usually acts. He's usually very outgoing, and he talks and laughs with the other students, inside the classroom and out. But these days he isn't smiling much. Normally Mohammed has lunch in the cafeteria, but today he isn't there eating. He often goes outside to smoke a cigarette, but he's not there smoking today.

Finally, someone asked Mohammed what was wrong. He explained that he is a Moslem (i.e., a follower of Islam). In the lunar calendar, it's now the month of Ramadan, so he's fasting. This month he isn't eating, drinking, or smoking during the daylight hours. The purpose of Ramadan is to teach discipline, and the fasting teaches compassion for people who are hungry and thirsty.

Everyone at Mohammed's school is glad that he's all right and that he's just trying to be a good Moslem.

Exercise 2 *(Focus 2)*

Using present progressive forms of the verbs from the list below, complete the dialogues about the following pictures. Be careful—some of them are short answers, some are negative, and others need a pronoun (*you, he, she,* etc.).

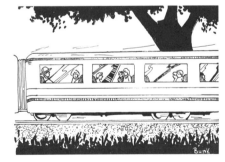

EXAMPLE: *Are they taking* a plane to the conference?

No, they're taking the train.

check	punch	type
die	quit	use
file	stand	water
fill	take	wear

1. _____ someone
   _____ those letters for me? I need
   them right now.
   Yes, Marcia _____ .

2. Who _____ my computer?
   Dave _____ .

3. Jody, _____
   those papers for Ms. Baxter?
   No, I _____ .
   Jim _____ .

4. That poor plant _____ .
   I know. That's why I _____ it.

5. _____ in or
   _____ out, sir?
   I _____ in.

6. Why _____
in line?
It's 7:00, time for the morning shift to begin.
They _____ in.

7. Where _____
out the application forms?
In Human Resources.

8. What _____ for the job
interview today?
I _____ my best dress.

9. Why _____ off his tie?
It's 5:00, time to quit working for the day.

10. Why _____ his job?

Because he hates working in that company.

Exercise 3 *(Focus 3)*

Complete the following with the **simple present** (e.g., *swims*) or the **present progressive** (e.g., *be + swimming*) forms of the verbs in parentheses. The first one has been done for you as an example.

Maria is an athlete who *is representing* (represent) her country in the Olympic Games. She **(1)** _____ (run) in the marathon, a 26-mile race. She usually **(2)** _____ (compete) in the triathlon, which means she **(3)** _____ (have) to run 10 kilometers, swim 1/4 mile, and ride a bicycle 25 miles. There's only a month to go before the Olympics, so Maria **(4)** _____ (train) hard to prepare. During regular training, she **(5)** _____ (swim) 1500 meters and **(6)** _____ (run) 5 miles, but during this pre-Olympic training, she **(7)** _____ (swim) less and she **(8)** _____ (run) more. She usually **(9)** _____ (work) out in the weight room an hour a day, but this month she **(10)** _____ (lift) weights for two hours a day, or double her normal time. Cross-country skiing is part of her winter training, but now that the weather permits, she **(11)** _____ (bicycle) and roller-blading, so that different muscle groups are exercised. Normally Maria **(12)** _____ (be) careful about her diet; she **(13)** _____ (eat) a limited amount of fat and a lot of fruits and vegetables. Now she **(14)** _____ (make) extra sure that she **(15)** _____ (eat) plenty of carbohydrates for energy. In addition, she **(16)** _____ (try) to get enough sleep. She **(17)** _____ (be) confident that she'll be prepared, mentally and physically, for the Olympics, and she **(18)** _____ (be) proud to be a part of this great event.

Exercise 4 (Focus 3)

Find a picture from a magazine or newspaper. Make sure it has activities that you can describe using the present progressive. Bring the picture to class, but don't show it to anyone. Sit with another student and describe your picture to your partner, without letting her or him see it. Then listen to your partner describe her or his picture. At the end of the activity, your teacher will collect all of the pictures and show them to the entire class. Can you choose the one that your partner described to you?

Exercise 5 (Focus 4)

Complete the following with the **simple present** or the **present progressive** form of the verbs in parentheses.

Stewart and Annie (1) _____ (be) college professors.

Right now it (2) _____ (be) spring break and they

(3) _____ (be) on vacation. They usually

(4) _____ (travel), but this year they (5) _____

(stay) home. They can't take a trip because they (6) _____

(have) too much to take care of. They have to fix things around the house and, besides,

they (7) _____ (think) it (8) _____

(be) cruel to leave their pets home alone. They have three indoor cats. They

(9) _____ (own [negative]) a dog, but their next-door

neighbor moved away and abandoned her dog, an Alaskan Malamute named Keno. They

(10) _____ (take) care of him, which

(11) _____ (be [negative]) easy because he

(12) _____ (be) a big dog and he

(13) _____ (be) afraid of people. Their former neighbor,

Theresa, mistreated the dog. As a result, every time Stewart or Annie

(14) _____ (reach) out a hand to pet Keno, he jumps

away and puts his head down. He (15) _____ (think) that

they're going to hit him. He (16) _____ (understand

[negative]) kindness; he (17) _____ (know) only cruelty.

Stewart and Annie (18) _____ (try) to be patient;

they (19) _____ (treat) him with love, hoping

that someday he will trust human beings again. They **(20)** _____
(take) Keno for a walk every morning and night, and they **(21)** _____
(play) with him in the yard every day. Out on the street, he **(22)** _____
(know [negative]) how to behave, so the couple **(23)** _____
(train) him. He **(24)** _____ (learn), little by little, and he
(25) _____ (begin) to trust them. They say that they
(26) _____ (look) for a home for him, a place where he
would have lots of room to run and people who **(27)** _____
(love) him. It **(28)** _____ (seem) to me that Keno already
(29) _____ (belong) to someone who
(30) _____ (love) him.

Exercise 6 *(Focus 5)*

Read the following sentences in the **simple present** and the **present progressive**. After each, check (✔) the column that indicates the meaning of the verb. The first column, state/quality, includes all of the **stative** verbs (i.e., those expressing emotion, perception, and cognition).

	State/ Quality/ Possession/etc.	Action/ Experience
1. Mark looks terrible today.	_____	_____
2. Do you think he has the flu?	_____	_____
3. Joe is looking up a word in the dictionary.	_____	_____
4. I think this apartment is too small.	_____	_____
5. I'm thinking about moving to a bigger place.	_____	_____
6. Daniel has a brand-new bicycle.	_____	_____
7. I'm having trouble with my car.	_____	_____
8. Pew! Something in the refrigerator smells awful.	_____	_____
9. Alonzo's at the perfume counter smelling the colognes.	_____	_____
10. Are you having a good time on your vacation?	_____	_____

11. Do you have time to help me?   _____   _____

12. Thank you. I appreciate your help.   _____   _____

13. Another girlfriend?! Who's he seeing now?   _____   _____

14. I don't see the logic of that argument.   _____   _____

15. Cynthia's having problems with her daughter.   _____   _____

UNIT 3

Be Going To and Will

Exercise 1 (Focus 1)

The sentences in the passage below are about the future. Underline the verb form (*will* or *be going to*) and circle the time expression that indicates the future.

EXAMPLE: <u>Will you marry</u> me, Loretta? I <u>will love</u> you (for the rest of my life.)

Nancy is engaged to be married. She and her fiancé, Tim, are trying to make their wedding plans, but Nancy's mother doesn't agree with them.

Nancy's mother: Now, I have it all planned, honey. We're going to go shopping for your wedding dress this weekend. Oh, you'll look so beautiful in a long, white dress!

Nancy: Mom, I'm not going to spend hundreds of dollars on a dress that I'll never wear again.

Nancy's mother: But your father and I will pay for it!

Nancy: No, Mother. I'm going to wear a simple dress.

Tim: And I'm going to wear a suit. No rented tuxedoes for me!

Nancy's mother: Now, what about the reception? We're going to have a big party and a band, aren't we?

Nancy: No, Mom. Tim and I want to have something more simple. Will you and Daddy have the reception at your house?

Nancy's mother: Well, it *is* traditional that the bride's parents pay for the reception. . . . I'm sure it'll be OK with your father. I'll ask him tonight.

Nancy: Thanks, Mom!

Exercise 2 (Focus 2)

Using the following predictions from fortune cookies, ask and answer a yes/no question about each, using *be going to* or *will*.

E X A M P L E : You will meet an interesting stranger.
Will I meet him at school?
No, you won't. You'll meet him at a party.

1. You will take a trip before the end of next month.

   _____

   _____

2. Soon you're going to meet someone special.

   _____

   _____

3. Someone will ask you to keep a secret.

   _____

   _____

4. You're going to receive some money.

   _____

   _____

5. You will live a long and happy life.

   _____

   _____

Exercise 3 (Focus 3)

For each of the following, decide on the best form to use: *be going to* or *will*.

According to sociologists, some parents in North America find it difficult to let their children go away to college in another city or state/province after they graduate from high school. It is customary to send young people away to the best possible university. North Americans feel that by going away to college, their children **(1)** _____ learn to be independent and self-sufficient, two qualities that are valued in their culture.

These traditional parents, however, are worried about their children's safety. They're afraid that something bad **(2)** _____ happen to their son or daughter

15

and they **(3)** _____ be [negative] able to protect them. Some parents don't think their children **(4)** _____ be successful on their own. They're afraid that the young people **(5)** _____ fail, that they **(6)** _____ be [negative] able to deal with everything, such as studying, doing laundry, and taking care of themselves. College officials and students say that these parents are also worried that their sons and daughters **(7)** _____ forget their family backgrounds and **(8)** _____ want [negative] to go back home.

Many young high school graduates, on the other hand, want to go away to college. Giselle Siu, a senior at Houston High School, said to her parents, "Look, I **(9)** _____ be 18 soon and legally I **(10)** _____ be able to leave, with or without your permission." Other students are more sensitive when they convince their parents. Alex Iavnoski, another high school senior who just received a letter of acceptance from the University of Iowa, told his parents, "I **(11)** _____ answer this letter right away and I **(12)** _____ say 'yes.' And with my scholarship, I **(13)** _____ save you money, too. Some day you **(14)** _____ be very proud of me." Still others don't even apply to colleges that are out of state. "My mom and dad are super strict. I know what they **(15)** _____ say, so I **(16)** _____ apply to the local community college," says Ramón Sierra.

Exercise 4 *(Focus 4)*

Complete the following sentences about your future. Use *be going to* for plans and intentions, and use *will* for predictions.

E X A M P L E : As a parent, *I'm never going to hit my children.*

1. As a parent, _____
2. After class today, _____
3. My horoscope today says that _____
4. After the end of this term/semester, _____
5. Next weekend, _____
6. After graduation, _____

7. Maybe on my next birthday, _____

8. Ten years from now, _____

9. My fortune cookie says that _____

10. On my next vacation, _____

Exercise 5 *(Focus 5)*

Complete the following, using *be going to, 'll, will* or *won't* as appropriate. In some of the sentences both *will* and *be going to* may be appropriate.

The Johnson family is having a family discussion.

Mr. Johnson: Rachel, David! Come here! We **(1)** _____ have a family meeting, and we **(2)** _____ talk about your responsibilities around the house.

Rachel: First can we talk about a dog? Oh, please, please, *please*, can we have a dog? My friend Amy Landusky and her family **(3)** _____ move to Japan, and they need to find a home for their dog, Scooby-Doo.

Mr. Johnson: You know a dog is a big responsibility. You have to feed it and walk it every day, and then there's the veterinarian. . . .

Mrs. Johnson: Remember what happened with the other pets? The bird? The rabbit? I had to take care of them without any help. I **(4)** _____ do that again!!

Rachel: But we're older now. I promise I **(5)** _____ walk the dog and feed him every day.

David: And I **(6)** _____ give him a bath every week.

Mrs. Johnson: And if we adopt this Scooby-Doo, who **(7)** _____ pay the vet's bills?

David: We **(8)** _____ use the money from our allowances to help. Oh, please, Dad? He can be a watch dog and protect the house when we're not here.

Mr. Johnson: Get me the phone. I **(9)** _____ call the Landuskys.

David: I **(10)** _____ get it! I **(11)** _____ get it for you, Dad!

Mr. Johnson: After we talk to the Landuskys, your mother and I **(12)** _____ discuss this some more, and then we **(13)** _____ decide.

17

Choose the <u>one</u> word or phrase that best completes the sentence.

1. _____ a job yet?
   - (A) Does he has
   - (B) Does he have
   - (C) Has he
   - (D) He has

2. Yes, Don _____ in construction; he is a carpenter.
   - (A) doesn't work
   - (B) is working
   - (C) isn't working
   - (D) work

3. All the carpenters on his crew _____ new houses.
   - (A) build
   - (B) builds
   - (C) is building
   - (D) will building

4. Don says, "A good carpenter _____ measures twice and saws once."
   - (A) always
   - (B) hardly ever
   - (C) never
   - (D) sometimes

5. This is the reason that Don _____ costly mistakes.
   - (A) always make
   - (B) doesn't make
   - (C) isn't making
   - (D) is always make

6. As soon as I finish doing this, I _____ visit a fortuneteller.
   - (A) 'm going to
   - (B) going to
   - (C) will
   - (D) will to

7. I _____ married next month, and I want to see what the stars say about my future.
   - (A) am going get
   - (B) 'm going to get
   - (C) will get
   - (D) won't get

8. Madame Flambé read my palm and said, "There _____ romance in your life."
   - (A) are going to be
   - (B) not going to be
   - (C) will be
   - (D) won't to be

9. According to the fortuneteller's crystal ball, I _____ someone new and fall in love.

    (A) going to meet   (C) will be meeting

    (B) 'm going to meet   (D) will meets

10. My fiancé found out. Now I have to promise him that _____ see Madame Flambé any more.

    (A) I'm going to   (C) I will

    (B) I'm not going to   (D) I won't

11. It used to be that an employee automatically retired at age 65, but nowadays people _____ off retirement, sometimes indefinitely.

    (A) are putting   (C) puts

    (B) is putting   (D) will put

12. It _____ that some people do it because they feel they need to keep busy; work has always been the center of their lives.

    (A) is seeming   (C) seems

    (B) seem   (D) will seem

13. These people don't know what to do with all the time that they now _____ during retirement.

    (A) are having   (C) has

    (B) is having   (D) have

14. Most of them _____ hobbies and they don't know how to spend all this leisure time.

    (A) don't have   (C) no have

    (B) haven't   (D) won't have

15. Other people continue working because of economic necessity—the government Social Security check _____ enough to live on.

    (A) is often   (C) often is

    (B) is seldom   (D) seldom is

Identify the one underlined word or phrase that must be changed in order for the sentence to be grammatically correct.

16. Most North American children begin to work at home, where they are having daily
                                    A   **B**
and/or weekly responsibilities, such as washing the dishes and feeding the dog.
                                         C   **D**

17. Children <u>receive</u> a weekly allowance <u>often</u>, which <u>is</u> a small amount of money, like a
                A   **B**   **C**
salary, in exchange <u>for</u> doing these household chores or jobs.
                D

18. The children <u>are using</u> this money <u>to buy</u> candy, soda, and other items <u>they</u> <u>need</u> for
             A   **B**   **C**   **D**
school.

19. Others <u>often</u> <u>save</u> <u>their</u> allowance and <u>making</u> bigger purchases: computer games, a pet,
       A   **B**   **C**   **D**
a musical instrument, or extra activities at summer camp.

20. The purpose of the allowance <u>is</u> to teach children the value of money, and to teach them
                              A
responsibility—when they <u>don't work</u> and do a good job, they <u>aren't</u> <u>receive</u> the money.
                       B   **C**   **D**

21. North Americans <u>often</u> <u>eat</u> out at fast-food restaurants because they <u>no</u> <u>have</u> time to
                  A **B**   **C** **D**
prepare food at home.

22. These restaurants <u>serve</u> almost anything from pizza to fried chicken to good old ham-
                A
burgers; some people <u>eat</u> inside, and others <u>stay</u> in their car and <u>buying</u> their food from
                 B   **C**   **D**
the drive-through window.

23. Some Americans <u>hardly</u> <u>never</u> <u>eat</u> at home; they <u>depend on</u> these inexpensive restaurants
              A   **B** **C**   **D**
for their meals.

24. For example, <u>never</u> my brother <u>prepares</u> his own food at home—he <u>always</u> goes out to
             A   **B**   **C**
fast-food restaurants and <u>eats</u> hamburgers and French fries.
                  D

25. <u>Are</u> you <u>think</u> it is healthy <u>to eat</u> that salty, processed, overcooked food?
  A   **B**   **C**   **D**

26. Karen and Steve, a modern young couple, <u>hardly</u> <u>never</u> <u>do</u> anything without a plan—
                              A   **B**
they <u>always</u> <u>talk</u> together about plans for their jobs, their home, and their family.
      C   **D**

27. Karen <u>is</u> expecting; next month she and Steve <u>are going to</u> have a baby. Their doctor
       A   **B**
<u>will say</u> that Karen <u>is having</u> a normal pregnancy.
  C   **D**

28. Karen and Steve <u>are knowing</u> what they're <u>going to</u> name the baby. If it's a girl, they'll
              A   **B**   **C**
name her Susan, and if it's a boy, they <u>will</u> name him Richard.
                     D

29. Karen <u>is following</u> all the doctor's instructions. She's <u>reading</u> a lot of books about preg-
         A   **B**
nancy and childbirth, and she <u>won't take</u> classes at the local hospital. When the time
                        C
comes, <u>she'll</u> be ready.
      D

30. It's time! Karen <u>is going to</u> have her baby very soon. She <u>will need</u> <u>to go</u> to the hospital
           A   **B**   **C**
right now, but Steve <u>can't</u> find the car keys.
              D

Past Progressive and Simple Past with Time Clauses

Exercise 1 *(Focus 1)*

The Gentleman Jewel Thief

Imagine that you are the following victims of the Gentleman Jewel Thief. Use the pictures to explain to the police what happened when the thief stole your jewels. Using the **past progressive** (e.g., *was/were talking*) or **simple past** (*talked*), write your answers to the questions below. The first one is done for you.

Case #1
Veronica Rio

Please...

last Sunday

E X A M P L E : Miss Rio, what were you doing at the time of the robbery?
I was having a drink at the Yacht Club.

1. Please describe the man who stole your jewels.

   _____

   _____

2. What did you do immediately after the thief stole your jewels?

   _____

   _____

Case #2
Eva Galor

last Saturday

3. Mrs. Galor, where were you and what were you doing at the time of the crime?

_____

4. Could you give us a description of the thief?

_____

5. Did the thief have a mustache?

_____

6. What did you do immediately after the thief stole your jewels?

_____

Case #3
Ruth Rox

last Friday

7. Mrs. Rox, what were you ladies doing when the thief stole your jewels?

_____

8. What did the thief look like?

_____

9. What was he wearing?

_____

10. Did he speak with an accent?

_____

11. What did you all do after he took your jewels?

_____

_____

Exercise 2 *(Focus 2)*

Imagine that you were at the bank when a robbery occurred. Test your observation skills by studying the following picture for two minutes. Then, using the **past progressive,** write as many sentences as you can about what was happening at the time of the robbery.

1. _____

2. _____

3. _____

4. _____

5. _____

6. _____

7. _____

8. _____

9. _____

10. _____

Exercise 3 *(Focus 2)*

Using the picture of the bank from Exercise 3, complete the following conversation between a detective and one of the tellers. Use the **past progressive** or the **simple past**, depending on the question.

1. Where was the manager at the time of the robbery? What was the manager doing?

   _____

2. Was the security guard there? What was he doing?

   _____

3. Were there any other employees in the bank? What were they doing?

   _____

4. Were any customers standing in line?

   _____

5. Please describe the person who was first in line.

   _____

6. Please describe the person who was last in line.

   _____

7. Was anyone acting suspiciously?

   _____

8. What time was it?

   _____

9. You said that there was a man outside the door. What was he wearing?

   _____

10. What were *you* doing at the time of the robbery?

   _____

Exercise 4 *(Focus 3)*

Using the pictures from Exercise 1, The Gentleman Jewel Thief, indicate if the following statements are true (T) or false (F). If the statement is false, rewrite it to make it true.

T F **1.** Veronica Rio kissed the thief when he stole her jewels.

_____

_____

T F **2.** Ms. Rio had a drink as soon as the thief took her jewels.

_____

_____

T F **3.** While Veronica was having a drink, the Gentleman Jewel Thief began to talk to her.

_____

_____

T F **4.** While Eva Galor was shouting, the thief took her jewels.

_____

_____

T F **5.** The thief was wearing sunglasses and a hat when the second robbery took place.

_____

_____

T F **6.** As soon as the thief took her jewels, Eva said "Thank you."

_____

_____

T F **7.** Mrs. Rox and her friends were playing bridge when the third crime took place.

_____

_____

T F **8.** As soon as the Gentleman Jewel Thief took their jewels, the ladies played bridge.

_____

_____

T F **9.** The thief was probably wearing a disguise when he committed these crimes.

_____

_____

T F **10.** While the Gentleman Jewel Thief was committing his crimes, he was rude to his victims.

_____

_____

Exercise 5 *(Focus 4)*

Rewrite the sentences from Exercise 4, changing the order of the clauses and the punctuation. The first one is done for you.

1. *When he stole her jewels, Veronica Rio ran after the thief.*
2. _____
3. _____
4. _____
5. _____
6. _____
7. _____
8. _____
9. _____
10. _____

Similarities and Differences

Exercise 1 *(Focus 1)*

Psychologists doing research on the brain find that some people use the right side of their brain more than the left side. Other people depend more on the left side of the brain when they have to solve a problem or learn something. A third group of people have no clear tendency; they use both sides of the brain fairly equally. The chart below shows some of the different characteristics of "right-brain" and "left-brain" people. Using the information from the chart, complete the sentences following it with the appropriate form of the **comparative** or **superlative**. The first one is an example.

Left-brain People	Right-brain People	Integrated
Logical, rational	Artistic, emotional	No clear preferences, flexible
Verbal—good speaking skills	Non-verbal	
Worry about details	Look at the "whole picture"	
Conservative	Liberal	
Want to be in control	Take risks	
Neat, organized	Seem unorganized, but know where things are	
Always on time or early	Rarely on time	
Competitive	Cooperative	
Good at algebra	Good at geometry	
Make lists of day's activities	Picture (i.e., "see in their mind") places, people, things they have to do	
After meeting someone for the first time, they remember the person's name	After meeting someone for the first time, they remember the person's face	
When shopping, they buy after reading labels, comparing prices	When shopping, they buy on impulse	
When explaining a plan, they do it orally	When explaining a plan, they prefer to use paper and pencil	

(Continued)

Left-brain People	Right-brain People	Integrated
Prefer to work alone	Outgoing—work well with others	No clear preferences, flexible
Enjoy sewing, chess	Enjoy skiing, swimming	
Like to plan trips	Like surprises	
Enjoy doing crossword puzzles	Enjoy fishing, running	
Like to fix things around the house	Like to rearrange furniture at home	

Left-brain People

E X A M P L E : They are _less_ emotional _than_ right-brain people.

1. They speak _____ skillfully _____ right-brain people.

2. They shop _____ carefully _____ people in the right-brain category.

3. The _____ competitive individuals of all are left-brain dominant.

4. They are _____, or more organized, _____ right-brain people.

5. They like to fix things _____ right-brain people do.

6. People in this group seem to be _____ impulsive _____ people in the other group.

Right-brain People

7. They are _____ artistic _____ left-brain people.

8. They probably have _____ friends _____ people in the other two categories.

9. They are _____ punctual _____ left-brain people.

10. They are _____ cooperative _____ people in the first group.

11. They like surprises _____ left-brain people do.

12. The _____ outgoing people of all the groups are in this category.

Exercise 2 *(Focus 1)*

Check (✔) your personal preferences in the chart below. Count the total number of check marks you have in each category to decide if you are left- or right-brain dominant. Compare your answers with those of your classmates. Then, using **comparative** and **superlative** forms, write sentences comparing yourself with the other members of the group.

Left-brain Dominant	Right-brain Dominant	No Preference
__ I'm logical and rational.	__ I'm artistic and emotional.	—
__ I'm verbal — I speak well.	__ I'm non-verbal.	—
__ I worry about details.	__ I look at the "whole picture."	—
__ I'm conservative.	__ I'm liberal.	—
__ I want to be in control.	__ I take risks.	—
__ I'm neat and organized.	__ I seem unorganized, but I know where things are.	—
__ I'm always on time or early.	__ I'm rarely on time.	—
__ I'm competitive.	__ I'm cooperative.	—
__ I'm good at algebra.	__ I'm good at geometry.	—
__ I make lists of my day's activities.	__ I picture (i.e. "see in my mind") my day's activities.	—
__ After I meet someone for the first time, I remember the person's name.	__ After I meet someone for the first time, I remember the person's face.	—
__ When shopping, I buy after reading labels and comparing prices.	__ When shopping, I buy on impulse.	—
__ To explain a plan, I prefer to speak.	__ To explain a plan, I prefer to use a pencil and paper.	—
__ I prefer to work alone.	__ I'm outgoing — I work well with others.	—
__ I enjoy sewing and/or chess.	__ I enjoy skiing and/or swimming.	—
__ I enjoy doing crossword puzzles.	__ I enjoy fishing and/or running.	—
__ I like to plan trips.	__ I like surprises.	—
__ I like to fix things around the house.	__ I like to rearrange the furniture at home.	—
__ **Total**	__ **Total**	__**Total**

E X A M P L E : *Susan is more artistic than I.*

I take more risks than Susan and Mark.

Mark is the most competitive person in the group.

1. _____

2. _____

3. _____

4. _____

5. _____

6. _____

7. _____

8. _____

9. _____

10. _____

Exercise 3 *(Focus 1)*

Using the pictures and information below, complete the sentences with the comparative or superlative form. When there is a word in parentheses, write the appropriate **comparative** or **superlative** form of that word.

Studious, quiet, likes computers and playing bridge, GPA = 4.0, an only child.

Norman

Athletic, outgoing, likes football and basketball, GPA = 2.0, four brothers and sisters.

Jerry

Artistic, antisocial, likes to smoke and drive fast cars, GPA = 1.0, an orphan.

Gary

Note: GPA = Grade-Point Average (on a 4-point scale, 4 is the highest grade and 0 is the lowest).

EXAMPLE: As little boys, Gary and Norman were probably _lonelier than_ Jerry.

1. Of the three boys, Norman studies _____, and Gary studies

   _____.

2. Norman's hair is _____ (long) Jerry's.

3. Norman's glasses are _____ (thick) Jerry's.

4. Norman's belt is _____ (wide) the other boys' belts.

5. Of the three boys, Jerry has _____ (big) feet.

6. Of the three, Gary is wearing _____ (tight) pants.

7. Gary's hair is _____ (curly) Jerry's.

8. Norman and Jerry probably drive _____ (carefully) Gary.

9. Gary and Norman are probably _____ (popular) Jerry.

10. Jerry probably has _____ (friends) the other two boys.

Exercise 4 (Focus 2)

Use the information below and the pictures from Exercise 3 to write sentences with **equatives** (_as . . . as_). Show the amount of difference or similarity as necessary.

EXAMPLE: Jerry/Gary/GPA/low

   Jerry's GPA is almost as low as Gary's.

1. Norman/Jerry/handsome

   _____

2. Gary/Norman/heavy

   _____

3. Norman/Gary/live/dangerously

   _____

4. Gary/Norman/smart

   _____

5. Norman/Jerry/tall

   _____

6. Norman/Gary/pants/tight

   _____

7. Norman/Gary/hair/straight

   _____

8. Jerry/Gary/grades/bad

_____

9. Jerry and Gary/Norman/grades/good

_____

10. Norman /Gary/play football/well

_____

11. Norman's house/Gary's house/quiet

_____

Exercise 5 *(Focus 3)*

Using the information from the chart in Exercise 1, complete the following sentences about Lois, a left-brain person, and Roy, a right-brain person. Write the correct form of the **comparative, superlative,** or **equative,** and any other words necessary to complete the sentence.

E X A M P L E : Lois's house is probably *cleaner than Roy's.*

1. Roy seems to be _____ organized _____ Lois.

2. Roy's closets probably aren't _____ neat
   _____ Lois's _____ .

3. Lois doesn't take _____ risks as Roy _____ .

4. Roy isn't _____ good at remembering names
   _____ Lois _____ .

5. Of all her friends, Lois is _____ mechanical and
   _____ artistic.

6. Roy isn't _____ conservative _____ most of
   his friends.

7. Lois doesn't have _____ friends _____ Roy
   _____ .

8. Lois probably doesn't like fishing _____ much
   _____ Roy _____ .

9. Roy doesn't talk _____ much _____ Lois
   _____ .

10. Roy likes decorating his house _____ Lois _____ .

Exercise 6 *(Focus 4)*

You are a car salesperson and you have to answer your customers' questions about the cars you sell. Be tactful and tell the truth, using *not as . . . as* or *not quite as . . . as* in your answers.

Cadillac Salesperson

EXAMPLE: Q: Is the Cadillac sporty? The Toyota is a nice, sporty little car.

A: *Well, the Cadillac isn't as sporty as the Toyota.*

1. Is the Cadillac more expensive than the Toyota? The Toyota is pretty inexpensive.

   _____

2. Is it easy to park? The Toyota is very easy to park.

   _____

3. Is it economical? The Toyota is super economical.

   _____

4. Is it dependable? The Toyota is very dependable.

   _____

5. Is the warranty good? The Toyota has an excellent warranty.

   _____

Toyota Salesperson

6. Can many people ride in the Toyota? A lot of people can fit in the Cadillac.

   _____

7. Is it dangerous? The Cadillac, because it's so big, is very safe.

   _____

8. Does it have a lot of features? The Cadillac has automatic windows, a CD player, and a security system.

   _____

9. Is it fancy? With the Cadillac, I can impress my friends.

   _____

10. Does it have a roomy trunk? With the Cadillac, I can carry a lot of things in the trunk.

   _____

Degree Complements

Exercise 1 (Focus 1)

The Ganter family has just moved to Nashville. They have three young children. They are looking for an older house for about $100,000, with at least four bedrooms, two bathrooms, and a large yard. Their realtor gave them the descriptions of the following houses. What do you think the Ganters said about each house? Write *enough, not enough,* or *too* as appropriate in the blanks.

Modern, beautiful home with all the conveniences: deluxe dishwasher, washer, dryer, side-by-side refrigerator and freezer. Three bedrooms, one bath. Small lot. $100,000.

EXAMPLE: There are *not enough* bathrooms.

1. It is _____ modern.
2. There are _____ bedrooms.
3. The yard is _____ large _____.
4. It is not _____ expensive.

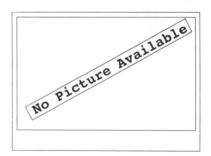

Built in 1926, this fixer-upper is loaded with space! Large lot. Four large bedrooms, two bathrooms. Old-fashioned breakfast room and pantry off the kitchen. $75,000.

5. There are _____ bedrooms.

6. There are _____ bathrooms.

7. The yard is large _____.

8. It is cheap _____.

Spacious four-bedroom, two-baths, city house is right in the center of action right on the Boulevard. Small yard easy to maintain with a pool. $125,000.

9. The house is large _____.

10. There are _____ bathrooms.

11. The yard is _____ small.

12. The street is _____ busy for kids.

13. It is _____ expensive.

Exercise 2 (Focus 2)

Penelope Picky's Perfect Party

Penelope Picky is having an elegant cocktail party this weekend. She's spending all day preparing, but she's very hard to satisfy. Complete the following appropriately, using *too, enough,* or *not enough* as necessary. The word list at the bottom of the exercise may help you, but don't limit yourself to those words. There are different ways to make meaningful responses for this exercise. Compare your answers with a partner's.

At the Caterer's

E X A M P L E : **Caterer:** What would you like to serve for dessert, Madam? Cheesecake?

Penelope Picky: No, *cheesecake is too fattening and you never serve enough*.

Caterer: Ice cream?

Penelope Picky: No, **(1)** _____.

Caterer:	Chocolate Mousse?
Penelope Picky:	No, (2) _____ _____.

Caterer:	Pastries?
Penelope Picky:	No, (3) _____ _____.

Caterer:	Flan?
Penelope Picky:	Yes, that will be perfect. It's not too sweet and it will be elegant enough.

At the Department Store Buying a Dress for the Party

Sales clerk:	What about this miniskirt?
Penelope Picky:	No, (4) _____ _____.

Sales clerk:	Perhaps you would prefer this elegant long dress?
Penelope Picky:	No, (5) _____ _____.

Sales clerk:	What about this leopard skin print?
Penelope Picky:	Definitely not, (6) _____ _____.

Sales clerk:	How about this one?
Penelope Picky:	Yes, (7) _____ _____.

Auditioning Musicians for the Party

Agent:	What about a rock band?
Penelope Picky:	No, (8) _____ _____.

Agent:	A string quartet?
Penelope Picky:	No, (9) _____ _____.

Agent:	I have a great country-western band.
Penelope Picky:	No, (10) _____ _____.

Agent:	What about a jazz quartet?
Penelope Picky:	Perfect, (11) _____.

softly	loudly	large
rich	fattening	cold
elegantly	wildly	short
long	seriously	silly
light	sophisticated	sexy
quietly	weird	tight
loose	stylish	sweet
musicians	dessert	calories
toppings	spots	time
space	money	

Exercise 3 *(Focus 3)*

Complete the following story with *too much, too many, too little,* or *too few.*

Lifestyles of the Extremely Rich

Robin Bird: Good evening folks, Robin Bird here with another fascinating episode of *Lifestyles of the Extremely Rich*. We're here today with Ms. Mercedes Benz at her fabulous home, San Coupe, in California. Ms. Benz, may I call you Mercedes?

Mercedes Benz: Certainly, Robin.

Robin Bird: Mercedes, do you really have 12 bathrooms here at San Coupe?

Mercedes: Well, yes Robin. I do have 12 bathrooms. Do you think that's

(1) _____ bathrooms?

Robin: No, of course not. But it must take quite a few servants to keep all those

bathrooms clean.

Mercedes: You're right, I never have enough servants. There are always **(2)** _____

servants around, and it takes **(3)** _____ energy to manage

all of them, but I get by somehow.

Robin: Let's talk about the grounds surrounding San Coupe. How much land do you own?

Mercedes: Well, I'm just not sure how much land I own, but I know I have **(4)** _____ grass to mow in one day, and I have three swimming pools. Unfortunately, I don't get enough exercise because I just bought two new cars, and now I have **(5)** _____ time to do much swimming.

Robin: How many cars do you own now?

Mercedes: Seven, one for each day of the week. Of course now I have the problem of **(6)** _____ garage space. But, that's what happens when you have **(7)** _____ cars.

Robin: Can you believe that, folks? Seven cars! Well, we have to go, but Mercedes, I want to thank you very much for sharing San Coupe with us. I hope we didn't take up **(8)** _____ of your time.

Mercedes: It was my pleasure, Robin. A woman like me can never get **(9)** _____ publicity. I get **(10)** _____ opportunities to show off San Coupe.

Exercise 4 *(Focus 4)*

The Ganter family went to see the "fixer-upper" house. Although the house was big enough and had a large yard, there were some problems. In fact, little Tommy Ganter renamed it the "junk house." Complete the list of problems the Ganters made. Use *too* to show that something is excessive, or more than enough. Use *very* to add emphasis.

Built in 1926, this fixer-upper is loaded with space! Extra large lot. Four large bedrooms, two bathrooms. Old-fashioned breakfast room and pantry off the kitchen. $75,000.

Problems with the Junk House

Kitchen

1. The appliances are _____ old and rusty.

2. The refrigerator is _____ moldy.

3. There are _____ few electric outlets. (only 1)

4. There are _____ many cockroaches. (5 cases of bug spray needed)

5. There is _____ little cupboard space. (only 1 cupboard)

Bedrooms

6. There are _____ few closets.

7. The roof is _____ leaky.

8. The bedrooms are _____ dirty. (3 inches of dust, hire a professional cleaner)

General

9. There are _____ many weeds in the yard.

10. The house is _____ old.

11. The electrical wires are _____ old. (rewire)

12. The house is _____ buggy. (has termites, ants, and roaches in every room)

13. It will be _____ hard to repair, but I think we can do it.

Exercise 5 *(Focus 4)*

Tell your partner two things you like and two things you don't like about where you live now. Be sure to use *too* and *very* in your description.

Choose the <u>one</u> word or phrase that best completes the sentence.

1. Maureen needed some money yesterday, so she _____ to the bank.
   (A) didn't go   (C) was going
   (B) has gone   (D) went

2. _____ Maureen was getting cash at an ATM, someone came up behind her and robbed her.
   (A) After   (C) Before
   (B) As soon as   (D) While

3. The thief _____ a T-shirt and blue jeans and had big tattoos all over his arms.
   (A) was wearing   (C) wearing
   (B) weared   (D) wore

4. _____ she realized what happened, Maureen ran to a phone, called the police, and reported the crime.
   (A) As soon as   (C) During
   (B) Before   (D) While

5. Luckily, she didn't have _____ money.
   (A) as much   (C) too little
   (B) enough   (D) very much

6. But Maureen still didn't have _____ to buy gas—she had to walk home.
   (A) cash enough   (C) too much cash
   (B) enough cash   (D) very cash

7. Later, the police told Maureen that she hadn't been _____. The thief had been standing near the bank and she should have noticed him.
   (A) as careful   (C) enough careful
   (B) careful enough   (D) less careful

8. The next day, someone _____ Maureen's purse, with all of her identification and credit cards, in a trash can.
   (A) find   (C) was finding
   (B) found   (D) was found

9. Thai food is hotter than Japanese food; by *hotter*, I mean _____.
   - (A) as spicy
   - (B) less spicy
   - (C) spicier
   - (D) the spiciest

10. It's _____ for people who don't like spicy food.
    - (A) as hot
    - (B) hot enough
    - (C) hotter
    - (D) too hot

11. It can be spicy hot like Indian food, but _____ as Indian food.
    - (A) as greasy
    - (B) less greasy
    - (C) more greasy
    - (D) not as greasy

12. Thai cuisine is _____ and more exotic than heavy French food.
    - (A) as light
    - (B) less light
    - (C) lighter
    - (D) more light

13. Like the French chefs, Thai cooks use _____ fresh herbs and spices.
    - (A) enough
    - (B) many
    - (C) too few
    - (D) too many

14. *Sateh* was originally Indonesian, but the Indonesian dish isn't _____ as the *sateh* from Thailand.
    - (A) as spicy
    - (B) less spicy
    - (C) quite spicy
    - (D) spicier

15. In my opinion, of all the world's cuisines, Asian cooking is _____.
    - (A) delicious
    - (B) more delicious
    - (C) most delicious
    - (D) the most delicious

Identify the <u>one</u> underlined word or phrase that must be changed in order for the sentence to be grammatically correct.

16. North American food, on the other hand, is <u>boring</u>; I think it's one of <u>the</u> <u>blander</u>, <u>least</u>
                                         A   **B**   **C**   **D**

    imaginative cuisines.

17. It uses too <u>little</u> spices and fresh <u>herbs</u> and <u>too</u> <u>many</u> canned and frozen ingredients.
                   A   **B**   **C** **D**

18. Other cooking around the world uses a <u>much</u> <u>wider</u> variety of herbs and spices <u>than</u>
                                           A   **B**   **C**

    the English <u>are</u>.
        D

19. North Americans eat a lot of processed and frozen food, which has chemicals and is <u>not</u>
    <u>**A**</u>
    as <u>healthful</u> <u>than</u> diets with <u>more</u> fresh, natural foods.
      B   **C**   **D**

20. They also eat at fast-food restaurants, which serve greasy food with <u>a lot of</u> calories.
                                              A
    That's part of the reason that North Americans are much <u>fatter</u> and <u>less</u> healthy <u>that</u>
                                       B   **C**   **D**
    other nationalities.

21. <u>Not all</u> North Americans eat fast food; some <u>enjoy</u> trying international food very much,
      A   **B**
    but to prepare that food at home isn't <u>enough convenient</u> <u>for them</u>.
                                    C   **D**

22. Yes, some <u>have started</u> to change their attitude about food, but <u>no enough</u>—the average
                 A   **B**
    North American <u>still</u> <u>eats</u> mashed potatoes, meat loaf, and Hamburger Helper.
                 C **D**

23. If North Americans borrowed <u>more</u> ideas <u>from</u> the cuisines of their various ethnic
                           A   **B**
    communities, they could have some of <u>a</u> <u>most</u> fascinating cooking in the world.
                               C **D**

24. Yesterday, <u>while</u> they <u>were driving</u> to work, Natasha and her husband, Yuriy, <u>were having</u>
              A   **B**   **C**   **D**
    an accident.

25. <u>While</u> Natasha <u>stepped</u> on the brake, the car that <u>was driving</u> behind them <u>hit</u> their car.
     A   **B**   **C**   **D**

26. The man who <u>was driving</u> behind them <u>was following</u> <u>too closely</u> <u>for</u> to stop.
             A   **B**   **C** **D**

27. <u>As soon</u> one of the neighbors <u>saw</u> the accident, he <u>called</u> <u>the</u> police.
      A   **B**   **C** **D**

28. An ambulance <u>came</u> right away <u>and</u> <u>was taking</u> Natasha and Yuriy <u>to the nearest hos-</u>
                A   **B** **C**   **D**
    pital.

29. <u>Was</u> Natasha and her husband <u>wearing</u> their seatbelts <u>when</u> the accident <u>occurred</u>?
     A   **B**   **C**   **D**

30. Yes, they were, and they feel very lucky that they weren't hurt <u>very much</u> and that the
                                                    A
    neighbors who <u>saw</u> the accident <u>enough cared</u> <u>to call</u> the police.
             B   **C**   **D**

UNIT 7

Giving Opinions and Advice

Exercise 1 *(Focus 1)*

Men and Women, What's Your Opinion?

Do you agree or disagree with the following statements? Check (✔) the appropriate column.

	Agree	Disagree
1. Men should help with the housework.	—	—
2. Women should not work outside the house.	—	—
3. Women should not be totally responsible for the child care.	—	—
4. Husbands ought to help their wives with the dishes.	—	—
5. Men and women should keep their traditional roles.	—	—
6. Boys shouldn't learn how to cook.	—	—
7. A college education ought to be available for both men and women.	—	—
8. Women should be encouraged to participate in athletics.	—	—
9. Wives ought to serve their husbands before they eat their own food.	—	—
10. A father should not help change the baby's diapers.	—	—
11. Women should learn how to change a tire.	—	—

Exercise 2 *(Focus 1)*

GROUP

Compare your answers from Exercise 1 with your classmates'. Discuss why you have certain opinions.

Exercise 3 *(Focus 2)*

Ask a person outside your class his or her opinions on the following questions and why he or she has that opinion. Write out his or her responses in complete sentences, using *should*, *ought to*, *shouldn't*, and *should not*.

E X A M P L E : *Omni believes that men should share in the housework because more women are working outside their homes.*

	Yes	No
1. Should men share in the housework? Why? _____ _____	—	—
2. Should female athletes earn as much money as male athletes? Why? _____ _____	—	—
3. Should women be combat soldiers? Why? _____ _____	—	—
4. Should husbands and wives share equally in raising children? Why? _____ _____	—	—
5. Should women be religious leaders? Why? _____ _____	—	—

Exercise 4 *(Focus 2)*

GROUP

Add up the results of all the surveys in your group. Then write sentences showing these results.

E X A M P L E : *Ten people think that men should share in the housework. Seven people think that men shouldn't share in the housework.*

Exercise 5 *(Focus 3)*

Ask Gabby

Advice columns appear in most North American newspapers. Readers write and ask for advice about problems they are having. Write four sentences of advice to the following people who are having problems. Use *should, should not,* or *ought to* to express your opinions.

Dear Gabby,

I moved to Canada from Korea three years ago. My mom says that I am forgetting my Korean heritage and I'm acting too much like a Canadian because I like curling and playing hockey with my friends. I'm not trying to be disrespectful to my mom. I just want to be like the other kids. What should I do?

Sincerely,
On Thin Ice in Calgary

1. _____

2. _____

3. _____

4. _____

Dear Gabby,

   I work all day as a cashier in a department store. When I come home my husband expects me to make his dinner and clean the house. Not only that, but my husband is a slob. When he comes home from work, he leaves his clothes all over and then just sits in front of the TV and drinks beer. What should I do?

Sincerely,
Worn Out in Waukegan

1. _____

2. _____

3. _____

4. _____

Dear Gabby,

   I'm a 25-year-old construction worker. I am very dissatisfied with my job. I've always wanted to help people. I'd like to study nursing, but all my friends say nursing is women's work. What should I do?

Sincerely,
A Fish Out of Water

1. _____

2. _____

3. _____

4. _____

Exercise 6 (Focus 4)

Rosario wants to be a doctor. Complete the following, using *should, shouldn't,* or *must* as appropriate. Different people may have different opinions about some of these, so be ready to justify your choices.

E X A M P L E : She *should* learn how to read X rays.

1. She _____ get high grades in college.

2. She _____ like biology.

3. She _____ study for at least seven years.

4. She _____ find some friends who also want to be doctors so they can support each other and study together.

5. She _____ apply for a scholarship.

6. She _____ be afraid of blood.

7. She _____ like to help people.

8. She _____ be able to work long hours.

9. She _____ take the Hippocratic Oath (a promise to follow a code of medical ethics).

10. She _____ work well under pressure.

11. She _____ smoke cigarettes while examining a patient.

Exercise 7 *(Focus 5)*

Giving Stronger Advice

Complete the following pairs of sentences with *should, ought to,* or *had better.*

EXAMPLE: Mother to daughter: "You <u>*should*</u> wear a warm jacket, or you'll catch a cold."

1. Parent to child: "You _____ eat your vegetables, or you won't get any dessert!"

2. One friend to another: "You _____ eat vegetables if you want to be healthy."

3. Teacher to student: "You _____ get a good grade on the final exam or you'll fail this class."

4. One student to another: "I agree we _____ study, but I'm ready for a break."

5. Worker to coworker: "To impress the boss, you _____ wear a tie to work."

6. Boss to worker: "You _____ be on time every day if you want to keep your job!"

7. Travel agent to tourist: "You _____ leave home early or you'll miss your flight, because there is a lot of traffic at that time."

8. One tourist to another: "You _____ visit the pyramids; they are a marvelous example of ancient architecture."

Write a sentence using *should, ought to,* or *had better* for each of the following situations.

1. Father to son: _____

_____

2. Student to teacher: _____

_____

3. Architect to builder: _____

_____

4. Prime minister to Parliament: _____

_____

Exercise 8 *(Focus 6)*

"Sure, Mom"

Victor's mother nags him about how he acts, and tells him something bad will happen if he doesn't follow her advice. Victor is on his way to college. This will be the first time he is away from home. His mother can't resist telling him the things he had better do at college one last time. Complete the sentences using the cues given with *had better, 'd better, had better not,* or *'d better not.*

E X A M P L E :   (write a letter) *You had better write a letter once a week or I'll come there and visit you.*

1. (study hard) _____

_____

2. (wash your clothes) _____

_____

3. (eat unhealthy food) _____

_____

4. (make me proud) _____

_____

5. (fail any classes) _____

_____

6. (pay the tuition money back) _____

_____

7. (stay out late)_____

_____

8. (remember how hard you worked to go to college) _____

   _____

9. (stay out of trouble) _____

   _____

10. (leave now) _____

    _____

Exercise 9 *(Focus 7)*

Should We Study?

It is the week before final exams and Victoria and Magalie are trying to decide what they are going to do today. Complete the following dialogue using *should* or *could* as appropriate. The first one has been done for you as an example.

Victoria: We <u>should</u> study for the biology exam.

Magalie: I know we **(1)** _____, but it's such a beautiful day.

               (2) _____ we go to the beach? We **(3)** _____ invite those cute guys who live in the next dorm.

Victoria: Sure, and we **(4)** _____ go swimming.

Magalie: Yeah, we **(5)** _____ play volleyball and get a great tan.

Victoria: I know—we **(6)** _____ get some hamburgers and have a barbecue!

Magalie: But if we go to the beach I **(7)** _____ buy a new bathing suit, because mine is getting old.

Victoria: OK, you get a new bathing suit and I'll get the food.

Magalie: Well, if we're going to have a barbecue, you **(8)** _____ get some more meat and we **(9)** _____ buy some charcoal.

Victoria: Wait, do you have any money?

Magalie: No.

Victoria: I'm broke too.

Magalie: So, what **(10)** _____ we do?

Victoria: We **(11)** _____ study for the biology exam.

Exercise 10 *(Focus 7)*

List three things you could do and three things you should do to study for your grammar test.

Could	Should
1. _____	1. _____
2. _____	2. _____
3. _____	3. _____

Exercise 11 *(Focus 8)*

For each of the following situations, use the words *should (not), ought to, could, must,* or *had better (not)* with the phrases given. There are many possible answers to each question since different people may have different opinions about some of these, so be ready to justify your choices. The first one has been done for you.

Abdul is getting a driver's license.

E X A M P L E : have an accident
> *He had better not have an accident while taking the road test.*

1. bring a passport or birth certificate

   _____

2. fail the written test

   _____

3. be nervous

   _____

4. practice parallel parking

   _____

Angelica is registering for college classes.

5. get her advisor's signature

   _____

6. register early

   _____

7. find out about the instructors

   _____

It's my mother's birthday.

8. buy her a gift

_____

9. bake a cake

_____

10. remind my father

_____

Ben and Sara are writing term papers.

11. start researching early

_____

12. type the paper

_____

13. turn the paper in late

_____

Diego is getting sick.

14. call the doctor

_____

15. get some rest

_____

16. take some aspirin

_____

Exercise 12 *(Focus 8)*

For each of the following situations, use the **modals** to give advice to the person with the problem.

E X A M P L E : José's wife snores and keeps him awake at night.

(should) *He should make a tape recording of her snoring so that she will believe him.*

(could) *José could sleep in another room.*

Matthew plays the guitar. He wants to be a rock musician.

1. (had better) _____
2. (could) _____

Bill got a speeding ticket.

3. (should) _____
4. (must) _____

Kristi has to tell her boyfriend she lost the necklace he gave her.

5. (ought to) _____
6. (could) _____

Geraldine forgot where she put her car keys.

7. (had better) _____
8. (could) _____

David's water pipes broke and there is water all over the kitchen.

9. (must) _____
10. (had better) _____

Lori lost her credit cards.

11. (must) _____
12. (should) _____

UNIT

8

Phrasal Modals and Modals of Necessity

Exercise 1 *(Focus 1)*

Indicate whether the following statements are true or false.

T F **1.** Before leaving on a trip abroad, or to another country, you should get a travel book with information about that country.

T F **2.** You shouldn't carry all of your money in cash, and you shouldn't put all your money in one place.

T F **3.** To enter some tropical countries, you mustn't have vaccinations and other shots to protect against tropical diseases.

T F **4.** When you check in at the airport, you don't have to pay extra if you have too much luggage.

T F **5.** You've got to pack your camera and passport in your suitcase.

T F **6.** During the flight, you mustn't smoke in the nonsmoking section.

T F **7.** When traveling abroad, you must learn to say *please* and *thank you* in the local language.

T F **8.** To drive in North America, you have to have a driver's license.

T F **9.** You should be able to carry all of your luggage by yourself.

T F **10.** When you're in a North American city, you mustn't ask about neighborhoods that you should avoid.

T F **11.** If you're lost in North America and you see a police officer, you should ask her or him for help.

Exercise 2 *(Focus 2)*

Complete the following conversation with the correct form of *must, have to,* or *have got to,* as indicated. Where no **modal** is indicated, answer with the correct pronoun and the auxiliary *do*. The first one has been done for you as an example.

Claudia and Andres, two foreign tourists, are renting a car. They're asking the agent about driving in the United States.

Andres: **(1)** *Do I have to* (I + have to) have a driver's license?

Agent: Yes, **(2)** _____.

Andres: What about Claudia? She has an international driver's license.

(3) _____ (she + have to) get another license?

Agent: No, **(4)** _____. She can drive here with an international license.

Claudia: What about seat belts? **(5)** _____ (we + have to) wear seat belts?

Agent: Yes, you **(6)** _____ (must) wear seat belts. It's the law in most states.

Andres: What **(7)** _____ (we + have to) do with that thing in the front seat of the car?

Agent: What thing? Oh, that's the litter basket. It's for litter: garbage, paper, and things that you want to throw away.

Claudia: Can't we just throw it out the window?

Agent: No, you **(8)** _____ (must [negative]) throw it out the window. There's a $500 fine for littering! You **(9)** _____ (have got to) keep everything inside the car.

Andres: **(10)** _____ (we + have to) drive on the left side of the road the way they do in England?

Agent: No!! You **(11)** _____ (must [negative]) drive on the left. Stay on the right.

Claudia: Are there any other laws that we should know about?

Agent: Well, if you're going to turn right or left, you

(12) _____ (have to) use your turn signal. On the highway, you **(13)** _____ (must) follow the speed limit, and if you're driving more slowly than the other cars, you

(14) _____ (have to) stay in the right lane. The left lane is for faster traffic. Obey the laws, or the police will stop you.

Exercise 3 *(Focus 3)*

Go back to Exercise 1 and rewrite the statements that you marked as false. Use the correct form of *should, must, have to,* or *have got to.*

_____

_____

_____

_____

_____

_____

_____

_____

_____

_____

_____

Exercise 4 *(Focus 4)*

Fill in the blanks below with the correct form of *have to* or *have got to,* whichever you think is more appropriate.

E X A M P L E : It's time for my yearly checkup. I _have to_ remember to call the doctor's office sometime this month.

1. I burned my finger while I was cooking. The first-aid book says that

   I _____ hold my finger under cold water.

2. She spilled hot oil all over her leg and foot. John _____ take her to the emergency room, now!

3. What _____ (Irene) do for her first-aid class?

   She _____ practice CPR (Cardiopulmonary Resuscitation).

4. His face is blue! We _____ check his throat to see what he's choking on.

5. There are jellyfish in the area. The lifeguard's telling Tommy that

   he _____ stay out of the water today.

6. Did that little girl drown? She stopped breathing. The lifeguard _____ start mouth-to-mouth resuscitation as soon as possible.

7. I cut my finger, and it's bleeding a little. What should I do? The neighbor, who's a nurse, says that you

   _____ wash the cut, and then put a bandage on it.

8. There's something in my eye again!
   Oh, Lee. You _____ stop wearing so much eye makeup.

9. The children _____ get their vaccinations before school starts.

Exercise 5 *(Focus 5)*

Some children are at a swimming pool with their grandmother. The lifeguard is shouting at the children, but they're not paying any attention. Their grandmother is repeating the lifeguard's instructions. In the spaces below, write what she says, using *must not* or *mustn't*.

E X A M P L E :   Walk! No running!

You mustn't run!   or   *You must not run!*

DIVING

1.   No diving in the shallow water!

_____

2.   You're not allowed to go in the deep water until you pass a swimming test.

_____

3.   Don't take beach balls in the water.

_____

4.   No pushing!

_____

5.   Get that radio away from the pool. No radios in the pool area!

_____

6.   Obey the rules! Stop breaking the rules!

_____

7.   Get that dog out of here! No pets allowed!

_____

8.   No eating or drinking in the pool area!

_____

9.   Stop hitting that little boy!

_____

Exercise 6 (Focus 6)

Look at the chart below on North American etiquette, and complete the sentences that follow it, using *have to, have got to, don't have to,* and *must not.*

	Personal Hygiene	Formal Introductions	Informal Introductions
Necessary	use deodorant wear clean clothes daily	smile shake hands say "Nice to meet you"	smile say "Hello"
Not Necessary	wear perfume, cologne	be very serious	shake hands
Prohibited	use too much perfume, makeup	kiss, hug	kiss, hug
	Tipping	**Table Manners**	**Clothing**
Necessary	leave the waiter/waitress a 15% tip	wait to eat until everyone is served	wear conservative clothes in business/law/religious services
Not Necessary	tip bad waiter/waitress leave a tip in a fast-food restaurant	accept offers of food	wear conservative clothes in other situations
Prohibited	tip government officials (e.g., police, customs)	make noise with mouth when eating	go barefoot (except at the beach)

E X A M P L E :   When you meet someone at a classmate's party, you *don't have to* shake hands.

1. North Americans don't have a lot of physical contact with each other, especially with strangers. When you meet people for the first time, you _____ kiss or hug them.

2. To make a good impression at a job interview, you _____ dress conservatively, and you _____ put on too much perfume.

3. North Americans like a good sense of humor. Even in business, a person _____ be formal and serious all the time.

4. For satisfactory service in a restaurant, it is customary to leave a 15% tip; but if the service is poor, you _____ tip the waiter.

5. To be accepted in North American society, you _____ take a bath every day and use deodorant.

6. You _____ go barefoot to a church, mosque, synagogue, or temple.

7. A business executive _____ shake hands when he meets someone for the first time.

8. On most college and university campuses, a student _____ dress up for classes; in fact, it's very casual.

9. Direct eye contact is important for North Americans. You _____ look at them directly and smile when you meet them, or they might think you're dishonest.

Exercise 7 *(Focus 6)*

Using the chart from Exercise 6 as a guide, write your own sentences about customs in your native country. *Use have to, have got to, don't have to,* and *must not.*

Necessary

1. _____

_____

2. _____

_____

3. _____

_____

Not Necessary

4. _____

_____

5. _____

_____

6. _____

_____

Prohibited

7. _____

_____

8. _____

_____

9. _____

_____

Exercise 8 *(Focus 7)*

Using the information from the chart in Exercise 6, complete the following conversation about Mary's trip to North America. Use *must, mustn't, have to,* or *do not have to,* in the present or past tense, as appropriate. The first one is done for you as an example.

Joe: Maria, how was your trip to America? You were there all summer, right?

Mary: Yes, I went there on an exchange program. I stayed with a family. It was great!

Joe: What was it like? Is it true that Americans *have to* take two showers a day or they don't feel clean?

Mary: No, that's not true.

Joe: Is it true that they are informal?

Mary: Yes, while I was there, I **(1)** _____ wear a dress or a skirt. Every day I wore shorts and sneakers, except one day when we went to court. The father of the family is a lawyer, and he says that in a courtroom, you **(2)** _____ dress more formally.

Joe: How was the food? Is it true that they eat hamburgers and hot dogs every day?

Mary: No, that's not true, but in the morning I **(3)** _____ eat cereal and drink American coffee.

Joe: Was the family rich?

Mary: No, they were middle class. They didn't have servants, so I **(4)** _____ help around the house. I **(5)** _____ clean my own room and help with the dishes. There was yard work, but I **(6)** _____ help with that.

Joe: What else **(7)** _____ do?

Mary: I **(8)** _____ walk the dog.

Joe: Is it true that in North America you **(9)** _____ treat pets almost like people?

Mary: Yes, the dog was a member of the family. The mother of the family said to me, "Mary, dogs are our friends. We **(10)** _____ love and respect them."

Joe: How about the people? Is it true that the people are nice?

Mary: Oh, yes! But one time I'm afraid that I offended some friends of the family. I asked a woman about her salary. The family told me, "Mary, you **(11)** _____ ask about a person's salary, age, or weight. It's too personal."

Exercise 9 *(Focus 8)*

Exchange your answers to Exercise 7 with a classmate (preferably someone from a different country and culture). Now imagine that you are planning a trip to that person's hometown. Write sentences about your plans, using *will have to, won't have to,* and *must not.* Share your answers with the class.

Necessary

1. _____

_____

2. _____

_____

3. _____

_____

Not Necessary

4. _____

_____

5. _____

_____

6. _____

_____

Prohibited

7. _____

_____

8. _____

_____

9. _____

_____

UNIT 9

Expressing Likes and Dislikes

Exercise 1 *(Focus 1)*

The students in Norma's class have a lot in common. Complete the following sentences about them, using *too* or *either* and the appropriate form of *do*.

EXAMPLE: Her son doesn't eat vegetables, and my daughter *doesn't either*.

1. Ramon studies Spanish, and Maria José _____.
2. I don't understand Greek, and my friends _____.
3. Ann doesn't like liver, and her sister _____.
4. Cheryl loves animals, and her children _____.
5. Elizabeth loves the English language, and my friends _____.
6. Maria doesn't like to write in English, and Dora _____.
7. Kathy listens to classical music, and I _____.
8. She doesn't listen to rock and roll, and I _____.
9. I like the teacher's new haircut, and most of the other students _____.
10. Roberto doesn't like it, and David _____.

Exercise 2 *(Focus 2)*

Rewrite the sentences from Exercise 1, changing *too* and *either* to *so* and *neither*.

EXAMPLE: *Her son doesn't eat vegetables, and neither does my daughter.*

1. _____

   _____

2. _____

   _____

3. _____

   _____

4. _____

_____

5. _____

_____

6. _____

_____

7. _____

_____

8. _____

_____

9. _____

_____

10. _____

_____

Exercise 3 (Focus 3)

Correct the mistakes in the following sentences.

                                                 does
E X A M P L E : Scott lives in Iowa, and so ~~is~~ Debbie.

1. I don't know how to windsurf, and my brother doesn't neither.
2. Sung can't type and neither Fathi can.
3. Mark went to the wrong restaurant, and Alonzo didn't too.
4. Bob didn't go sailing, and either did Irene.
5. Mayumi hasn't been here long, and Sato isn't either.
6. Cynthia was in class yesterday, and you was too.
7. You was sick last week, and so was Sheila.
8. Lee won't come with us, and either will Ed.
9. Maureen has a cute boyfriend, and so has Patty.
10. Jim had a cold last week, and Taylor had too.

Exercise 4 *(Focus 4)*

Match the sentences in the first column with the appropriate **rejoinder phrase** in the second column. Remember to use the inverted form to emphasize the speaker's feelings about the topic. The first one is done for you as an example.

1. Oliver went to the union   I am too.
   meeting last night.

2. His boss wasn't there.   I did too.

3. My boss thinks everything   Mr. Fagin does too.
   is fine at work.

4. He wasn't happy to hear   Mr. Fagin hasn't either.
   about the meeting.

5. He hasn't been very professional.   Mr. Fagin wasn't either.

6. I felt bad about what he said   Neither does Mr. Fagin.
   to us.

7. I think it's wrong not to say   Neither was Mr. Fagin!
   what you think.

8. Well, I'm for the union.   Neither will Mr. Fagin.

9. My boss doesn't like unions.   So can I!

10. My manager won't be happy   So did I.
    if we vote for a union.

11. Oliver can do what he wants.   So do I.

Exercise 5 *(Focus 5)*

Complete the conversation below with **rejoinder phrases**, such as *So do I* or *I don't either*, or **hedges**, such as *Kind of* or *Sort of*.

In writing class

Brian: Did the teacher like your composition?

Daniel: Well, **(1)** _____.

Brian: What grade did you get?

Daniel: I got a "C".

Brian: **(2)** _____. Actually, I'm happy. I don't usually pass.

Daniel: **(3)** _____. I'm terrible at writing. Conversation class is more fun. I'm better at speaking.

Brian: **(4)** _____. How about reading? Do you like Reading class?

Daniel: **(5)** _____. I don't really like the teacher.

Brian: (6) _____.

Daniel: I'm tired of studying English.

Brian: (7) _____.

Daniel: I like my other classes a lot better.

Brian: What other classes?

Daniel: I'm taking music classes.

Brian: Really?! (8) _____! I'm taking Music Theory and guitar lessons. How about you?

Daniel: I'm taking Theory and voice lessons. Who's your Theory teacher?

Brian: Professor Kaplan.

Daniel: Do you like the class?

Brian: (9) _____. It's difficult. I like the other class better. Do you like your voice lessons?

Daniel: (10) _____. Music Theory is my favorite class.

Exercise 6 (Focus 6)

Psychologists have found that some people use the right side of their brain more than the left side, and other people depend more on the left side of the brain when they have to solve a problem or learn something. In Unit 5, there is an exercise on right- and left-brain preferences. The list below shows some additional characteristics of "right-brain" and "left-brain" people. Check (✔) the sentences which are true for you. Then add up the number of check marks in each column to see if you are left-brain dominant, right-brain dominant, or balanced. Are your results the same as before?

After you finish, circle all of the **gerunds** in the lists.

Left-brain	Right-brain
___ I have a place for everything and a system for doing things. ___ I enjoy sewing. ___ I enjoy chess. ___ I understand contracts, instruction manuals, and legal documents. ___ I like to plan and arrange the details of a trip. ___ I like to collect things. ___ I enjoy working on home improvements.	___ I enjoy swimming. ___ I enjoy skiing. ___ I enjoy bicycling. ___ I am good at thinking up new ideas. ___ I enjoy photography. ___ I can understand charts and diagrams. ___ I like to relax and just do nothing. ___ I enjoy dancing. ___ I like to paint or sketch. ___ I postpone making telephone calls. ___ I enjoy fishing.

(Continued)

Left-brain	Right-brain
__ I enjoy writing.	__ I enjoy running.
__ I play bridge.	__ I like to sing in the shower.
__ I like to read.	__ I enjoy rearranging my furniture and decorating my home.
__ I play a musical instrument.	__ When shopping, I buy what I like.
__ I enjoy doing crossword puzzles.	__ After meeting a person for the first time, I remember the person's face.
__ After meeting a person for the first time, I remember the person's name.	
__ Before buying something, I read the label and compare prices.	
__ I'm good at speaking.	
__ I like competing with others.	
__ **Total**	__ **Total**

Exercise 7 *(Focus 6)*

Complete the following sentences. Use a gerund in your answer.

E X A M P L E : I hate *ironing*.

1. One of my favorite hobbies is _____.

2. I enjoy _____ and _____.

3. I can't stand _____.

4. I like to talk about _____.

5. I'm good at _____.

6. When I was little, _____ was something that I loved to do.

7. I usually postpone _____.

8. I feel good after I finish _____.

9. I feel bad after I finish _____.

10. Two Olympic sports are _____ and _____.

Exercise 8 *(Focus 6)*

GROUP

Working in groups of three or four, compare your answers to Exercises 6 and 7. Take turns reading a statement about yourself. The students who have the same answer respond with the appropriate **rejoinder phrase** (e.g., *I do too, So do I, I don't either,* or *Neither do I*).

TOEFL® Test Preparation
Exercises · Units 7–9

Identify the one underlined word or phrase that must be changed in order for the sentence to be grammatically correct.

1. Frank hasn't seen that new movie about skiing and I haven't neither.
          A   **B**   **C** **D**

2. After he finish washing the dishes, Fred wants to go for a bike ride. So do I.
         A   **B**   **C** **D**

3. I can understand why he loves working with computers, and his mother can't either.
    A   **B**   **C** **D**

4. Hilda enjoys to be outside in her yard gardening, and Florence does too.
            A   **B**   **C**   **D**

5. She stays in good physical shape by jogging and to run. Her boyfriend does too.
                        A   **B**   **C** **D**

6. I think that if a person lives in North America, she or he should learn how to swim.
                                                     A

   When my parents were in college, they must to pass a swimming test in order to grad-
        B   **C**   **D**
   uate.

7. But at most colleges nowadays, a student doesn't have to do that as a requirement for
                                 A   **B**

   graduation. You're right, I didn't had to do that when I was in college.
                    C   **D**

8. Ought I learn to be safe around water? Yes, you should. You ought to take water safety
    A   **B**   **C**

   classes from the Red Cross. The first rule in water safety is that you shouldn't swim
                                                D
   alone.

9. The second rule in water safety is that to save a drowning person, you mustn't try to
                                                    A

   swim to him. You ought to throw something. You also could to reach for the drowning
                  B   **C** **D**

   person with something like a pole or towel.

10. Children should learn about water safety. They have got to go near the water alone; an
             A   **B**   **C**

    adult should always be with them.
          D

11. I have a toothache. What I should do? Well, you could take some aspirin, but it is
     A   **B**   **C**

    probably better to see the dentist.
          D

12. I know I had better not be afraid to go the dentist, but I always get nervous sitting in
          A   **B**   **C**

    the dentist's chair.
      D

13. The dentist <u>makes</u> me feel anxious and <u>so does his</u> assistant. Let me see what it <u>looks</u>
    A   B   C
    like. Oh, that tooth looks painful, and <u>so the tooth</u> next to it.
    D

14. You <u>must</u> <u>see</u> the dentist right away! To avoid painful toothaches you <u>could</u> brush your
    A B   C
    teeth and <u>use</u> dental floss.
    D

15. You <u>ought to</u> <u>visit</u> a dentist twice a year and your children <u>should</u> <u>so.</u>
    A   B   C D

Choose the <u>one</u> word or phrase that best completes the sentence.

16. I don't like shopping, and Nancy _____.
     (A) doesn't either   (C) isn't either
     (B) doesn't too   (D) isn't neither

17. Bobby has a pair of skates, and _____.
     (A) Irene has too   (C) so does Irene
     (B) Irene is too   (D) so has Irene

18. Kelly _____ to go fishing, and so does Mike.
     (A) does like   (C) is like
     (B) doesn't like   (D) likes

19. Robin loved the movie, and _____.
     (A) I lived too   (C) so did I
     (B) I didn't   (D) so do I

20. Bart enjoys _____ antiques.
     (A) collect   (C) collecting
     (B) collects   (D) to collect

21. In North America classrooms, the students _____ stand when the teacher enters
    the room.
     (A) don't have to   (C) not must
     (B) haven't got   (D) no should

22. In some classes, students may eat, but they _____ smoke; it's the law.
     (A) don't have to   (C) mustn't
     (B) haven't got   (D) shouldn't

23. During class the teacher can have something to drink and the students _____.
     (A) will too   (C) can too
     (B) are too   (D) drink too

24. However, students _____ stand up and walk around the class while the teacher is talking.

    (A) oughtn't to   (C) shouldn't

    (B) have got to   (D) will have to

25. When I was a student, I _____ treat my teachers with more respect than students do nowadays.

    (A) didn't have to   (C) had to

    (B) had got to   (D) must have

26. _____ do anything to prevent heart disease?

    (A) Have got I   (C) Should I

    (B) Ought I to   (D) Had better I

27. The Heart Association gives some advice: you _____ eat healthy food, without too much fat or cholesterol.

    (A) should   (C) had better not

    (B) must   (D) could

28. If you don't want to die of heart disease, you _____ have a low-fat diet, get more exercise, and get frequent check-ups from a doctor.

    (A) shouldn't   (C) could

    (B) had better   (D) had better not

29. If you feel chest pains, you _____ see a doctor as soon as possible, or your life may be in danger.

    (A) could   (C) must

    (B) had better not   (D) ought to

30. Finally, you _____ try to eliminate stress.

    (A) do not have to   (C) couldn't

    (B) shouldn't   (D) could

Want and Need

Exercise 1 (Focus 1)

Match the first half of the sentences in the first column with the second half in the second column. The first one has been done for you as an example.

1. Human beings need

2. Sam needs to eat his vegetables, but he

3. Rick's doctor says that

4. Mark wants to watch TV,

5. He wants some dessert, but

6. Maggie's at summer camp and she misses her family;

7. Imelda wanted to buy some new shoes,

8. Mercy wants to take an aerobics class, but

9. Jon wants to travel, but

10. Pets, like people,

11. Connie's doctor says that she's too thin and

but his mother says that he needs to do his homework.

even though she had 200 pairs in her closet.

food, shelter, and clothing.

he doesn't really need it.

he needs to lose fifty pounds.

her advisor says that she doesn't need the credits.

his girlfriend wants to stay home.

need love and attention.

needs to gain ten pounds.

she wants to go home.

wants some ice cream instead.

Exercise 2 (Focus 2)

Read the statements below and decide what the person *needs/needed* or *wants/wanted*. The list at the end includes some possible answers.

E X A M P L E : The gas gauge in the car reads "E" for empty.
          We *need some gas*.

1.   Where would you like to go on vacation?

     I _____.

2. This table is too heavy for him to move alone.

    He _____.

3. Nicole has too many emotional problems to handle alone.

    She _____.

4. What can I bring you for dessert?

    I _____.

5. What's wrong with little Susie? Doesn't she like visiting her Aunt Ethel?

    Well, Susie really _____.

6. Why the sad face? You got a "B" on the test!

    I _____.

7. Victor would like to go to Syria. They require a visa to enter the country.

    He _____.

8. Gidget wants a Coke from the vending machine, but she has only a $20 bill.

    She _____.

9. What's the matter? You have a healthy baby boy.

    I _____.

10. That light is too high for Florence to reach.

    She _____.

an "A"	go to Australia	some help
a girl	go to Disneyworld	some ice cream
a ladder	some change	some professional help
a visa		

Exercise 3 *(Focus 3)*

Fill in each blank with the correct form of *want* or *need*. Remember to make the appropriate changes when the sentence is negative. The first one has been done for you as an example.

Philip: Oh, Hillary. I *want* you. I **(1)** _____
_____ you. I can't live without
you. What do I **(2)** _____
to do to make you marry me?

Hillary: Philip, I can't marry you. I don't love
you. I **(3)** _____ to
hurt you, Philip, but I love another man.

69

Philip: Hillary, I can give you the world. What do you **(4)** _____?
Diamonds? A yacht? Money? Servants?

Hillary: Servants?! I **(5)** _____ any servants. I know how to cook
and clean. And I **(6)** _____ or **(7)** _____ your
money. I have my own money. I have my own job.

Philip: What do you **(8)** _____, then?

Hillary: I **(9)** _____ to marry William. I love William. I
(10) _____ to spend the rest of my life with someone I
don't love.

Exercise 4 (*Focus 3*)

Complete the following, using the correct form of *want* or *need*. Remember to make the
appropriate changes when the sentence is negative.

Generous Jane

Selfish Sally

1. When Generous Jane was a little girl, she _____ to share every-
    thing.

2. When Selfish Sally was a little girl, she _____ to share anything.

3. When Jane's friends _____ help, she helped them.

4. When Sally's friends _____ help, she didn't help them.

5. When Jane's mother _____ her to go to bed, she went to bed.

6. Sally went to bed when *she* _____ to go to bed. She never listened
    to her mother.

7. When her friends _____ to borrow something, Generous Jane al-
    ways lent it.

8. Selfish Sally didn't lend anything to anyone. Nobody even _____
    to ask her!

9. When Jane played games with her friends, she _____ to win. She
    just _____ to have fun.

10. When Sally played games, she always _____ to win.

70

Present Perfect

Exercise 1 *(Focus 1)*

Listed below are some important events in the life of Carmen Alvarez, but the events are not in the order in which they happened. Write the numbers of the events in the correct order on the time line. If the event is something which began in the past and continues to the present, write it out on the lines below the time line. The first one has been done for you.

1. She has volunteered at a hospital for one year.
2. She will go to medical school.
3. She was born in Monterrey, Mexico, in 1969.
4. She learned English at New Mexico Technical Vocational Institute.
5. She hasn't become a doctor yet.
6. She has lived and studied in Albuquerque, New Mexico, since 1987.
7. She is studying biology, chemistry, and mathematics at the University of New Mexico.
8. Since she was a child, she has dreamed of becoming a doctor.
9. She learned how to take a blood sample.
10. She graduated from high school in 1986.
11. She will be a pediatrician.

Past	**Present**	**Future**

←————————————————————————————————————→

1. She has volunteered at a hospital for 1 year.

_____

_____

_____

Exercise 2 *(Focus 1)*

Using the previous exercise as a model, make a time line of your life. Be sure to include, past, present, and future events as well as events which began in the past and continue to the present.

_____

_____

_____

_____

_____

_____

_____

_____

_____

Past   **Present**   **Future**

←——————————————————————————————→

Events which began in the past and continue to the present

_____

_____

_____

_____

Exercise 3 *(Focus 2)*

In order to donate blood, you must answer several questions about your medical history. Complete the following dialogue between a blood donor and the interviewer using the correct form of the verb in the **present perfect**. The first one has been done for you as an example.

1. Interviewer: How long *has it been* (it be) since you ate?

    Donor: I _____ (not eat) anything since breakfast.

2. Interviewer: _____ (you give) blood before?

    Donor: Yes, I _____ (give) blood many times.

    Interviewer: Really? How long _____ (it be) since you last donated blood?

Fifth Annual
Blood Drive

Give for the Heart of It!

Donor:	I _____ (not donate) blood for a year.
3. Interviewer:	_____ (you have) any serious illnesses?
Donor:	No, I _____ (have) any illnesses.
4. Interviewer:	_____ (you be) in the hospital in the past five years?
Donor:	No, I _____ (not be) hospitalized.
5. Interviewer:	_____ (you travel) abroad?
Donor:	Yes, _____ (go) to South America.
Interviewer:	How long ago was that?
Donor:	I was in South America in 1990, but I _____ (live) in the United States since then.
Interviewer:	Thanks for answering the questions. Now will you please roll up your sleeve and we'll take your blood.

Exercise 4 (Focus 2)

PAIR

Copy down the interviewer's main questions from the previous exercise.

1. _____
2. _____
3. _____
4. _____
5. _____

Take turns role-playing the interview with a partner. Answer the questions using your own experiences and history.

Exercise 5 (Focus 3)

Complete the dialogue on the next page by writing *since* or *for* in the blanks. The blank in the sign in front of the castle has been filled in for you as an example.

Count Dracula: Good evening, Mr. Stoker. Welcome to the Count Dracula Blood Bank. So nice of you to come. We would like to take your blood, but first we want to see if you're our type. Would you answer a few questions?

Stoker: Well, uh, I guess so.

Count Dracula: How long has it been **(1)** _____ you arrived in Transylvania?

Stoker: I just arrived. I've only been here **(2)** _____ two hours.

Count Dracula: Oh! Have you had time to explore the castle?

Stoker: Well, I've walked around a little **(3)** _____ I got here. The castle is interesting, but that back room is full of bats.

Count Dracula: Yes, we've had that problem **(4)** _____ the castle was built. That reminds me, how long has it been **(5)** _____ you flew at night?

Stoker: What? I haven't flown at night **(6)** _____ the last year. I'm afraid of the dark.

Count Dracula: Well, perhaps we can help you with that problem. How long has it been **(7)** _____ you've been in a cemetery?

Stoker: These are the strangest questions I've ever heard. I guess the last time was in March. Yes, it's been three months **(8)** _____ I was in a cemetery.

Count Dracula: Very good. Finally, Mr. Stoker, have you given blood before?

Stoker:	Yes, but I haven't donated **(9)** _____ the last six months.
Count Dracula:	Wonderful! Because you've answered all our questions, we've decided you're a perfect victim—I mean candidate. Please roll down your collar.

Exercise 6 *(Focus 4)*

Look at the personnel file for Mercy Hospital. Which doctor has worked at the hospital the longest? Which nurse?

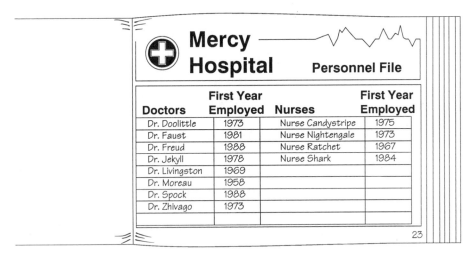

Doctors	First Year Employed	Nurses	First Year Employed
Dr. Doolittle	1973	Nurse Candystripe	1975
Dr. Faust	1981	Nurse Nightengale	1973
Dr. Freud	1988	Nurse Ratchet	1967
Dr. Jekyll	1978	Nurse Shark	1984
Dr. Livingston	1969		
Dr. Moreau	1958		
Dr. Spock	1988		
Dr. Zhivago	1973		

Use the information from the personnel files to make statements with the words given below.

E X A M P L E : Dr. Zhivago/since *Dr. Zhivago has worked at Mercy Hospital since 1973.*

1. Dr. Moreau/for _____

   _____

2. Dr. Jekyll/since _____

   _____

3. Dr. Zhivago and Nurse Nightengale/for _____

   _____

4. Dr. Faust/for _____

   _____

5. Nurse Rachet/for _____

   _____

6. Dr. Doolittle/since _____

   _____

7. Dr. Spock/for _____

   _____

8. Nurse Candystripe/for _____

_____

9. Nurse Shark/since _____

_____

10. Dr. Livingston/since _____

_____

11. Dr. Freud and Dr. Spock/since _____

_____

Exercise 7 (Focus 5)

Rewrite these sentences using the **present perfect** and *since* or *for*.

E X A M P L E :   Does she work for Air Canada? Did she begin to work there six years ago?
Has she worked for Air Canada for six years?

1. Do you like ice cream? Did you like it when you were a child?

_____

2. She sings with the Toronto City Opera. She started singing there three years ago.

_____

3. He is an accountant. He became an accountant in 1985.

_____

4. Our parents enjoy playing tennis. They began playing tennis when we went to college.

_____

5. Grandma doesn't drive anymore. She stopped driving when she turned 85.

_____

6. Are your aunt and uncle in Victoria, British Columbia? Did they go there last week?

_____

7. Nathan plays baseball every day. He started playing two years ago.

_____

8. Their house is a wreck. It was destroyed when Hurricane Andrew struck.

_____

9. She is in the library. She started to study three hours ago.

_____

10. It isn't raining; it stopped raining at 5:00 A.M.

_____

Present Perfect and Simple Past

Exercise 1 *(Focus 1)*

Decide if the following verbs should be in the **simple past** or the **present perfect**. Then circle the correct form.

Captain Michael Johnson, a pilot, is retiring this year. He (was / has been) one of the best commercial airline pilots in the world. He (began / has begun) working for Western Airlines 35 years ago. In the beginning of his career, he (flew / has flown) only domestic flights, but later on the company (told / has told) him to fly internationally. Captain Mike, as the flight attendants call him, (flew / has flown) around the world many times. He (met / has met) a lot of people and (saw / has seen) a lot of different places. In one year he (went / has gone)

to India, Egypt, and Greece, where he (saw / has seen) the Taj Mahal, the pyramids, and the Acropolis. In addition, he (did / has done) a lot of exciting things. On one trip, in 1980, he (jumped / has jumped) from an airplane with a parachute, and on another trip he (rode / has ridden) in a submarine. But his life (wasn't / hasn't been) easy. In 1976 his plane almost (crashed / has crashed); he (had / has had) to make an emergency landing. Ten years ago, he (had / has had) cancer, but Captain Mike (fought / has fought) the cancer and (won / has won). All in all, he (was / has been) very lucky, and so (were / have) we here at Western Airlines. We're going to miss you, Captain Mike.

Exercise 2 *(Focus 2)*

Using the words below, write sentences with the **present perfect** (*have* + **past participle**).

EXAMPLE: I / not meet a famous person

I haven't met a famous person.

1. John / not eat ants

   _____

2. Helena / be to Hong Kong?

   _____

3. Adam and Kristen / see a penguin

   _____

4. you / ride a camel?

   _____

5. I / not catch any fish

   _____

6. Loren / not shoot a gun

   _____

7. I / have a pet snake

   _____

8. you / go to the Galápagos Islands?

   _____

9. Larisa and Dora / stand in line for more than an hour

   _____

10. you / do something crazy?

    _____

Exercise 3 (Focus 3)

Have you ever done these things? Using the words below and the present perfect, write sentences about your experiences. If you haven't ever done the activity, use *never* or *not + ever*.

E X A M P L E : study Chinese

   I have studied Chinese.

   or *I haven't ever studied Chinese.*

1. find a wallet in the street

   _____

2. fly in a helicopter

   _____

3. fight in a war

   _____

4. break a bone

_____

5. give blood

_____

6. know a person from Greenland

_____

7. have a car accident

_____

8. wear snowshoes

_____

9. build anything

_____

10. travel to other countries

_____

Exercise 4 (Focus 4) PAIR

Using the verbs from Exercise 3, ask your partner if she or he has ever done those activities. If she or he has, ask the appropriate questions about the activity (_when, where, . . . ?_). Write down all of your partner's answers. When it's your partner's turn to ask the questions, use the sentences from Exercise 2.

1. _____

2. _____

3. _____

4. _____

5. _____

6. _____

7. _____

8. _____

9. _____

10. _____

Identify the one underlined word or phrase that must be changed in order for the sentence to be grammatically correct.

1. The native people of Northern Canada and Alaska have participated in dog sled races
    **A** **B**

   since more than 500 years.
    **C** **D**

2. The Inuit people has used dog sleds as their main source of transportation since settling
    **A** **B** **C** **D**

   in the northern parts of North America.

3. The sled dogs have working as faithful beasts of burden, carrying people and equipment
    **A** **B** **C**

   from place to place.
   D

4. In the past, every Inuit family wants a dog sled team because this was the only source
    **A** **B** **C**

   of transportation over the frozen land.
   D

5. The use of sled dogs as the primary means of transportation have declined since the
    **A** **B** **C** **D**

   invention of the snowmobile.

6. One of the most famous sled dog races, the Iditarod Trail, covers more than 1,000 miles
    **A**

   of Alaskan wilderness; it have challenged competitors and their dogs for many years.
    **B** **C** **D**

7. I have wanted seeing this race for a long time, but I never had the opportunity.
    **A** **B** **C** **D**

8. Last year, I have seen this great race for the first time. I was there at the finish line in
    **A** **B** **C** **D**

   Nome, Alaska.

9. Have you never eaten Indian food? No, I haven't.
    **A** **B** **C** **D**

10. I have had Indian food several times, but I didn't had it in a long time. I think you
     **A** **B** **C** **D**

    would like it.

11. Yes, I think I would. I've always wanted to try Indian food, but not ever had the chance.
     **A** **B** **C** **D**

12. Indian food is famous for its curried vegetables. I have ate curried eggplant and curried
     **A** **B** **C** **D**

    beans.

13. That sounds great. Let's go eat now. I need some lunch; I haven't have anything to eat
     **A** **B** **C** **D**

    all day.

14. I need to look up the address of the Indian restaurant. I haven't being there in a while.
$\quad$ $\underset{A}{\text{to look}}$ $\underset{B}{\text{up}}$ $\quad$ $\underset{C}{\text{haven't}}$ $\underset{D}{\text{being}}$

14. I need <u>to look</u> <u>up</u> the address of the Indian restaurant. I <u>haven't</u> <u>being</u> there in a while.
$\qquad\quad$ **A** $\quad$ **B** $\qquad\qquad\qquad\qquad\qquad\qquad\qquad\qquad$ **C** $\quad$ **D**

15. I think I'll enjoy this. I <u>haven't</u> <u>eaten</u> out <u>since</u> a while and I <u>want</u> a new taste experience.
$\qquad\qquad\qquad\qquad\qquad$ **A** $\qquad$ **B** $\qquad\quad$ **C** $\qquad\qquad\quad$ **D**

Choose the <u>one</u> word or phrase that best completes the sentence.

16. _____ to Smoky Mountain National Park since it has been improved?
    - (A) You been
    - (B) Were you
    - (C) Have you been
    - (D) Did you go

17. No, but I want _____ back there.
    - (A) going
    - (B) to go
    - (C) go
    - (D) went

18. I _____ camped in such a beautiful national park since I was in Yellowstone National Park in Wyoming.
    - (A) no
    - (B) didn't
    - (C) haven't
    - (D) don't

19. The wilderness is breathtakingly beautiful, but the campsites are rough; they _____ few of the amenities of home.
    - (A) have had
    - (B) have
    - (C) haven't
    - (D) has

20. There are wild animals in the park, and campers _____ be aware of the bears, who like to steal the campers' food.
    - (A) have
    - (B) have had
    - (C) had
    - (D) have to

21. To discourage the bears, all campers _____ to put away all food and make sure the lids are placed tightly on the garbage cans.
    - (A) needs
    - (B) want
    - (C) need
    - (D) wants

22. While you're camping there, you _____ to worry about what to do.
    - (A) didn't need
    - (B) didn't want
    - (C) don't need
    - (D) don't want

23. Park rangers _____ many hiking trails since the park opened.
    - (A) have developed
    - (B) will develop
    - (C) are developing
    - (D) develop

24. Rangers have protected the natural beauty of the Great Smokies National Park _____ it was created.
    - (A) for
    - (B) since
    - (C) when
    - (D) that

25. In the last decade, computers _____ an important part of everyday life.
   - (A) have become
   - (B) will become
   - (C) have became
   - (D) has became

26. _____ computers have been readily available for home use, it has become more important to become computer literate.
   - (A) For
   - (B) Since
   - (C) When
   - (D) At the time

27. Schools are teaching all children to be computer literate because in the future everyone will need _____ these skills.
   - (A) to have
   - (B) having
   - (C) have
   - (D) can have

28. Almost every part of our lives _____ computerized—work, school, the government, and even the grocery store over the past few decades.
   - (A) had
   - (B) have been
   - (C) was
   - (D) has been

29. Since I _____ in college, I _____ a computer to help me write my papers.
   - (A) 've being . . . 've using
   - (B) was . . . 've used
   - (C) 've been . . . 've used
   - (D) 've been . . . used

30. Yesterday, I _____ a computer to write my term paper.
   - (A) have used
   - (B) used
   - (C) has used
   - (D) have been using

Present Perfect Progressive

Exercise 1 *(Focus 1)*

Read the following story. Underline the words which show that the activities were in progress recently in the past. The first one has been done for you as an example.

The Henderson family is on their way home from a week of camping. What <u>have they been doing</u> for the last week? Well, Mrs. Henderson <u>has been cooking</u> over a campfire. She enjoys cooking outdoors. But she has also been washing the dishes in a bucket. She doesn't like that very much.

The whole family has been living in a tent. They haven't been sleeping in regular beds. Instead, they have been sleeping in sleeping bags.

The boys, Eric and Todd, have been very busy. They have been hiking and mountain climbing with their dad in the mountains. Also, they have been swimming in the cool mountain lakes.

Rachel Henderson has been hiking too, but she also has been going horseback riding. Rachel loves horses.

Finally, they have been having a contest to see who can find the most varieties of birds. So everyone has been birdwatching.

After the busy week they have been having, the Hendersons are glad to go home and have a vacation from their vacation.

Exercise 2 *(Focus 1)*

Make a list of three things you have been doing since you arrived at your class. Write complete sentences.

1. _____

2. _____

3. _____

Exercise 3 (Focus 2)

Complete the following dialogue with the correct form of the verb in parentheses. The first one has been done for you as an example.

Mom: What _have you been doing_ (you do)?

Lee: Nothing. We **(1)** _____ _____ (not do) anything.

Mom: Are you sure? You **(2)** _____ _____ (make) lots of noise out here and you **(3)** _____ (run).

Chris: We **(4)** _____ (play) baseball, Mom.

Lee: Yes, we **(5)** _____ (play) catch.

Mom: **(6)** _____ (you play) on the vacant lot next door?

Chris: Yes, we **(7)** _____ (practice) with Aaron.

Mom: **(8)** _____ (you do) anything besides throwing and catching the ball? I hope you **(9)** _____ (not hit) the ball with a bat. You could break one of Mr. Smith's windows if you do that.

Lee: I **(10)** _____ (catch), but Aaron **(11)** _____ (hit) the ball.

Mom: You didn't break a window, did you?

Chris: Sorry, Mom.

Mom: I **(12)** _____ (tell) you that you would get into trouble some day. I guess we had better go see Mr. Smith.

Exercise 4 *(Focus 3)*

Reggie is arriving at baseball practice late. His teammates have already been practicing for 10 minutes. Use the information in the picture to complete the sentences about what Reggie's teammates have been doing. If you are unsure about the activities, the words at the bottom of the page will help you.

E X A M P L E : Duke and Babe *have been swinging bats*.

1. Ted _____.
2. Stan and Yogi _____.
3. Willie _____.
4. Ozzie _____.
5. Sandy and Cy _____.
6. Whitey _____.
7. Mickey _____.
8. Roberto _____.
9. Duke _____.
10. The grounds keeper _____.

run	drink water	do push-ups
throw	pitch	hit
catch	cut the grass	chew gum
stretch	swing bats	

Exercise 5 (Focus 3)

Using the picture in Exercise 4, ask your partner what the players have been doing when Reggie arrives.

EXAMPLE: A: Has Satchell been doing push-ups?
          B: No, he hasn't. He's been pitching.

Exercise 6 (Focus 4)

Read the following sentences. On the line before each sentence write **1** or **2**. Write:

1. If the sentence **emphasizes** that the action is **without interruption**.
2. If the action is finished but **when it finished is unknown**.

EXAMPLE: <u>1</u> The Klebert family has been working since early this morning to clean their house for a party.

—— Mrs. Klebert has cleaned the kitchen.
—— She's washed and dried all the dishes and put them away.
—— She has also wiped all the counters, and swept and mopped the floors.
—— Deborah Klebert has been straightening up the bedrooms.
—— She has changed the sheets and made the beds.
—— Ben Klebert has been cleaning the bathrooms for the last hour.
—— He has scrubbed the sinks and toilets.
—— He's also changed the towels.
—— Mr. Klebert has been working on the living room.
—— He's been vacuuming and dusting and making sure that everything is in its right place.
—— They've been hurrying to finish in time for the party. I hope they are not too exhausted to enjoy themselves at their party.

Exercise 7 (Focus 4)

Think about the activities that you have done already today. Write one sentence about your own activities for each of the examples below.

1. Something you have done without interruption.

   _____

2. Something you have finished, but don't tell exactly when it finished.

   _____

Exercise 8 (Focus 5)

Fill in the blanks with the appropriate form of the verb. The first one has been done for you as an example.

Joel: Jimmy, you look terrible. What _have you been doing_ (you do) recently?

Jimmy: I **(1)** _____ (sleep [negative]) well lately.

Joel: **(2)** _____ (you be) sick?

Jimmy: I **(3)** _____ (not feel) sick. My allergies

(4) _____ (be) acting up a little for the last

week, that's all.

Joel: **(5)** _____ (something bother) you at school

recently?

Jimmy: Well . . . not really.

Joel: Tell me what **(6)** _____ (worry) you.

Jimmy: I **(7)** _____ (think) about my grammar exam

for the last week.

Joel: Why?

Jimmy: We **(8)** _____ (study) the present perfect pro-

gressive and I'm not sure if I understand it.

Joel: **(9)** _____ (you study) hard and

(10) _____ (ask) for help when you need it?

Jimmy: Yes, I **(11)** _____ (memorize) the form of the

present perfect progressive and **(12)** _____ (try)

to remember its meaning and how to use it correctly since the teacher taught it

to us.

Joel: You **(13)** _____ (worry) about nothing. I'm

sure you'll do fine.

Exercise 1 *(Focus 1)*

Match the captions with the pictures.

___ What would you like to do tonight?
I'd like to go dancing.
Wonderful!

___ It looks like you have a flat tire.
Would you like some help?

___ The style is perfect, but it's a little tight.
Would you like me to find a larger size?

___ I'm not sure I know how to get there.
Would you like Dave to show you the way?

___ Would you like to sample our flavor of the month, fudge ripple?
Yes, please.

___ The extension is 3876; would you like me to connect
you to that department?

___ Would you like to pay cash or is this a charge?

___ Would you like some ketchup with those fries?
Thanks.

___ Would you like to make a deposit or withdrawal? This is a deposit.

Exercise 2 *(Focus 2)*

Pierre Eclare has just become the new assistant manager of the Dew Drop Inn Cafe. He is trying to make the atmosphere a little more polite and sophisticated, so he is listening to how the waitresses talk to the customers. Read the dialogue between Wanda the waitress and her customers, Phil and Emilie. Then rewrite the dialogue using more polite forms.

Wanda: Good morning. Where do you want to sit? Do you want a table by the window?

Phil: Yes, that would be fine.

Wanda: Do you want some coffee?

Phil: Yes, please, two coffees.

Wanda: Sugar or cream in that coffee?

Emilie: Sugar for me, please.

Wanda: There's your coffee. Do you want to order now?

Phil: Yes, I guess we do.

Wanda: What do you want?

Emilie: I'll have eggs and French toast.

Wanda: How do you want your eggs?

Emilie: Fried, but not too well-done.

Wanda: Do you want me to tell the cook to make them over easy?

Emilie: Yes, please.

Wanda: And you, Sir? Do you want eggs, too?

Phil: Yes, I'll have the cheese omelette with hash browns.

Wanda: Do you want anything else?

Phil: Yes, some orange juice.

Wanda: Here's your breakfast. Do you want some ketchup for those hash browns?

Phil: Yes, please.

Wanda: Do you want anything else?

Phil: Just the check, please.

Wanda: _____

Phil: Yes, that would be fine.

Wanda: _____

Phil: Yes, please, two coffees.

Wanda: _____

Emilie: Sugar for me, please.

Wanda: _____

Phil: Yes, I guess we would.

Wanda: _____

Emilie: I'll have eggs and French toast.

Wanda: _____

Emilie: Fried, but not too well-done.

Wanda: _____

Emilie: Yes, please.

Wanda: _____

Phil: Yes. I'll have the cheese omelette with hash browns.

Wanda: _____

Phil: Yes, some orange juice.

Wanda: _____

Phil: Yes, please.

Wanda: _____

Phil: Just the check, please.

Exercise 3 (*Focus 3*)

Read the descriptions of Marc Antony and Cleopatra's first date and another date a year later. Write out their dialogue using *would you like* or *do you want*, as appropriate. Marc Anthony's first line has been written for you as an example.

First Date	
Marc Antony	**Cleopatra**
1. asks Cleopatra for a date	2. accepts the offer
3. asks Cleopatra what kind of restaurant she wants to go to	4. says she prefers French or Italian
5. asks what movie Cleopatra wants to see	6. tells him which movie she wants to see

Marc Antony: (1) *Would you like to go out with me this weekend?*

Cleopatra: (2) _____

Marc Antony: (3) _____

Cleopatra: (4) _____

Marc Antony: (5) _____

Cleopatra: (6) _____

| **One Year Later** | |
Marc Antony	Cleopatra
7. asks Cleopatra if she wants to stay home and watch pro wrestling	8. says she prefers to go country-western dancing
9. asks if she wants to order out for pizza	10. says she prefers to get Chinese food
11. asks her if she wants to go bowling and eat at the bowling alley instead	12. accepts

Marc Antony: (7) _____

Cleopatra: (8) _____

Marc Antony: (9) _____

Cleopatra: (10) _____

Marc Antony: (11) _____

Cleopatra: (12) _____

Exercise 4 *(Focus 4)*

Write a dialogue for the following situations. Be sure to consider the politeness of the situation. The first one has been started for you.

1. A flight attendant on an airplane offers a passenger lunch. The passenger isn't hungry, but would like something to drink.

   Flight attendant: Would you like some lunch?

   Passenger: _____

2. A father offers to help his son with his homework. The son really needs help.

   _____

   _____

3. The attendant in a gas station offers to wash a car's windshield. The driver accepts.

   _____

   _____

4. A lady with two small children and a stroller is having difficulty getting off a bus. You offer to help her. She accepts.

   _____

   _____

5. An elderly man is standing on a street corner looking lost. Another man offers to help him. The elderly man explains that he is waiting for a bus.

   _____

   _____

6. Your best friend stops by on a hot August day. You offer her or him a glass of homemade lemonade. She or he gladly accepts.

   _____

   _____

7. A friend of Patricia's cousin has just arrived in Canada from Guatemala. Patricia offers to show her the sights of Montreal. The friend declines because she has an important business meeting.

   _____

   _____

8. Deb's husband strained his back playing basketball. Deb offers to give him a back rub. He accepts.

   _____

   _____

UNIT

15

Requests and Permission

Below are some situations in which requests are commonly made. For each situation, make a request using *can*, *could*, *will*, *would*, or *please*, as appropriate.

E X A M P L E : You're driving to a party with a friend. You're not sure exactly where the party is, but you have a map in the glove compartment. You say to your friend: *Would you please look for a city map in the glove compartment? I'm not exactly sure where the party is.*

1. You're not sure which bus goes to the beach. You see a man waiting at the bus stop. You say: _____

_____

2. After you find out which bus to take, you want to know how often it stops here. You turn to the man again and say: _____

_____

3. When you come home from shopping, your arms are full of groceries. You see your neighbor standing next to the front door of your apartment building. You say: _____

_____

4. You have to be at work a half hour early tomorrow. Your husband/wife always gets up before you and wakes you up. You say to him or her: _____

_____

5. You are looking for your seats in a theater. You know your seats are in the balcony, but you're not sure how to get there. You see an usher and you say: _____

_____

6. You've invited a friend to go on a picnic. You know she has a daughter the same age as your daughter. You want her to bring her daughter along. You say: _____

_____

7. It's your turn to pick up the kids after soccer practice, but you have some work to finish at the office before you go home. You call up your spouse and say: _____

_____

8. You're giving a dinner party. Suddenly you realize you are out of eggs and you need eggs for your dessert. You call up your neighbor and say: _____

_____

9. You're trying to find the immigration building. You know it's nearby. You go up to a friendly looking woman and say: _____

_____

Exercise 2 (Focus 2)

The following are some of the requests that Aunt Esther made, but Caro refused. Complete the following dialogue with a **"softening" phrase** and a **reason**. The first one has been done for you as an example.

Aunt Esther: Oh, hello, dear. I'm so glad to see you. Could you please set the table for me? I'm running a little late.

Caro: *I'm sorry, I can't. I don't know where the dishes are.*

Aunt Esther: Well, can you stir the monkey-brain soup while I set the table then?

Caro: _____

Aunt Esther: OK. Could you please put the squid next to the cactus salad?

Caro: _____

Aunt Esther: I need a serving dish for the broiled eel. Will you get me that long thin platter?

Caro: _____

Aunt Esther: Oh, I've left the salt in the kitchen. Would you please get it for me? I really don't like fish eyes without salt.

Caro: _____

Aunt Esther: Would you please cut up the cactus for the kids, dear?

Caro: _____

Aunt Esther: Can you lend me your fork, please? I've dropped mine on the floor.

Caro: _____

Aunt Esther: Could you please pass the rattlesnake meat?

Caro: _____

Aunt Esther: Would you hold this platter of iguana while I serve some?

Caro: _____

Aunt Esther:	Well, dear, you didn't eat very much tonight. I suppose you're on a diet. Could you please bring the chocolate-covered ants for dessert?
Caro:	_____
Aunt Esther:	Well, will you help me with the dishes?
Caro:	_____
Aunt Esther:	I'm sorry you have to go so soon. Could you stay a little longer?
Caro:	_____

Exercise 3 (Focus 3)

Hanna, a flight attendant, is on a flight to Great Falls, Montana with the Polite family. Mr. and Mrs. Polite and Peter and Polly Polite are always making requests of Hanna. Write Hanna's positive responses to the Polite family's requests.

Mrs. Polite

Could you get me a pillow?

Would you bring me some more sugar for my coffee, please?

Can you show me where the bathrooms are?

Mr. Polite

Could I have another drink?

Will you take away my food tray?

Could you bring me a news-paper, please?

Hanna

_____

_____

_____

_____

_____

_____

Would you tell me where to catch my connecting flight to Joe, Montana?

_____

Peter Polite

Could I have a deck of cards, please?

_____

Would you get me a blanket?

_____

Polly Polite

Could I please have a *Glamour* magazine?

_____

Will you turn down the air? It's blowing my hair.

_____

Would you get me some ear-phones?

_____

Exercise 4 *(Focus 4)*

Below are some situations in which permission is commonly asked. For each situation ask for permission using *could, can, may,* or *would you mind if,* as appropriate.

E X A M P L E : You get a chance to meet your favorite singer. Ask for permission to take her or his picture.

Would you mind if I took your picture?

1. A young girl wants to spend the night at a friend's house this weekend. She asks her mother for permission.

    _____

2. Gus is at a formal dinner party and needs to leave the table for a minute. He asks the hostess for permission.

    _____

3. You are at a friend's house. You would like to smoke, but you're not sure if it is allowed. Ask permission to smoke.

    _____

4. You've got a friend from Japan coming to visit. You'd like your friend to see what an American school is like. Ask permission from your teacher to bring your friend to school.

    _____

5. Your community organization is having a special summer program for children. Ask the owner of the drug store for permission to put one of your posters about the program in his store window.

_____

6. You have a doctor's appointment at 4:00. Ask your boss for permission to leave work early.

_____

7. Your classroom is getting a little hot and stuffy. Ask your teacher for permission to open the window.

_____

8. You find an interesting magazine at the library. You're not sure if you can check out magazines. Ask the librarian for permission to check it out.

_____

9. You park your car by an office building. You are not sure if parking is permitted. Ask the security guard for permission to park there.

_____

Exercise 5 (Focus 5)

The following are the reactions of each person who was asked permission for something in Exercise 4. Using the answers from Exercise 4 and the information below, write the responses. If permission is refused, use a **"softening" phrase** and tell why it is refused.

E X A M P L E : The singer says "yes."

Sure, you can take my picture.

1. Her mom says "no."

_____

2. The hostess says "yes."

_____

3. Your friend doesn't allow smoking.

_____

4. Your teacher says "yes."

_____

5. The owner gives permission.

_____

6. Your boss doesn't give permission.

_____

7. Your teacher says "yes."

_____

8. The librarian says "no."

_____

9. The security guard says "no."

_____

Identify the one underlined word or phrase that must be changed in order for the sentence to be grammatically correct.

1. I <u>has</u> <u>been trying</u> to get to South Mall <u>for</u> the last 10 minutes. Do you know what bus
    A   **B**   **C**
  I <u>have to take?</u>
     D

2. You <u>can't</u> get a bus downtown from here. <u>Do</u> you <u>like</u> me to <u>show</u> you the way to the
     A   **B**   **C**   **D**
  bus stop?

3. Yes, <u>would you</u> <u>please help me?</u> I <u>have been living here not</u> long and I <u>can't figure out</u>
       A   **B**   **C**   **D**
  the bus system.

4. Yes, <u>I would.</u> You <u>have to</u> <u>take</u> either the number 3 or 16 bus. The bus stop is there,
      A   **B**   **C**
  <u>across</u> the street.
   D

5. Thank you. I <u>can't</u> believe it. I <u>have</u> <u>been</u> <u>stood</u> on the wrong side of the street.
           A   **B** **C** **D**

6. Deb, Jim <u>is</u> in town. <u>Would you mind</u> if he <u>comes</u> to the party tonight?
       A   **B**   **C**   **D**

7. No, that <u>would</u> be great. I'd love to have him come. I <u>haven't</u> <u>been seeing</u> him for a
        A   **B**   **C**   **D**
  long time. Is he all right?

8. He <u>has</u> <u>worked</u> hard lately, and I think <u>he's</u> under too much stress.
    A   **B**   **C**
  He <u>could use</u> some rest.
     D

9. <u>Do</u> he <u>been</u> <u>doing</u> a lot of <u>traveling</u> for his job?
  A   **B**   **C**   **D**

10. Yes. He <u>has</u> <u>been spending</u> a lot of time on airplanes. Lately, he <u>has</u> <u>been going</u> to New
        A   **B**   **C**   **D**
  York and Chicago several times.

Choose the one word or phrase that best completes the sentence.

11. Could you carry this notebook for me? Sure, I _____.

    (A) can   (C) would

    (B) could   (D) may

12. What do you have in that box? What have you _____on?

    (A) be work   (C) being worked

    (B) been working   (D) working

13. This is my science project for school. Recently, I _____the quality of water in different parts of the city.

    (A) have been testing   (C) has been testing

    (B) will have tested   (D) will test

14. _____me to carry something else? It might make things easier.

    (A) May   (C) Would you like

    (B) Couldn't   (D) Could

15. Thanks, I'd appreciate that. I wouldn't want these to break. I _____these samples for a week.

    (A) 've been studied   (C) has been studying

    (B) had studied   (D) 've been studying

16. _____lend me your calculator? I left mine at home.

    (A) May you   (C) Would you like

    (B) Could you   (D) Might you

17. _____but the batteries in my calculator have gone dead. It doesn't work.

    (A) Yes,   (C) No problem,

    (B) I'd like to,   (D) Sure,

18. I _____my homework and now I want to check my answers.

    (A) have been finishing   (C) have finished

    (B) will have finished   (D) finish

19. _____to compare your answers with mine? That way we could both check our homework.

    (A) Do you like   (C) May you like

    (B) Would you like   (D) Could you like

20. That's a great idea. _____you move your desk over here so we can compare answers?

    (A) May   (C) Could

    (B) Do   (D) Did

Past Habitual

Exercise 1 *(Focus 1)*

Circle T if the statement is true, and F if the statement is false.

T F   **1.** People used to use candles and gas lamps because they didn't have electricity.

T F   **2.** Before electricity, people used to put a big block of ice in the icebox; today we use a refrigerator.

T F   **3.** Before electricity, people used to use batteries for power.

T F   **4.** Before the invention of the car, people used to ride the bus.

T F   **5.** People used to walk much more than they do now.

T F   **6.** There didn't use to be as much violent crime as there is now.

T F   **7.** People used to know much more about nutrition than they do now.

T F   **8.** Big families used to be much more common than they are now.

T F   **9.** People used to live longer than they do now.

T F   **10.** There didn't use to be a big drug problem.

Exercise 2 *(Focus 2)*

Using the words below, ask and answer questions with the correct form of *used to*.

E X A M P L E :   You/have long hair?

Did you use to have long hair?

Yes, I used to have very long hair.

1. Where/you/live?

_____

_____

2. When you were a little boy/girl, what/you/play?

_____

_____

3. When you were in elementary school, what/you/do after school?

_____

_____

4. When you were very young,/your parents/read to you?

_____

_____

5. What bad habit/you/have?

_____

_____

6. What/you/look like?

_____

_____

7. Who/be your best friend?

_____

_____

8. You/live in the city?

_____

_____

9. Where/you/go on vacation?

_____

_____

10. You/wear glasses?

_____

_____

Exercise 3 (*Focus 3*)

Fill in the blank with the correct form of *used to* or *anymore*.

My grandmother complains about how things have changed, and she says that life
(1) _____ be better.

Families aren't families the way they **(2)** _____ be. Everyone's divorced. If a husband and wife are having problems with their marriage, they don't stay
together **(3)** _____. And mothers **(4)** _____ stay
home and take care of their children, but not **(5)** _____. Everyone's
working. No one has time for children **(6)** _____.

And the cars! No one walks **(7)** _____; everybody drives. We
(8) _____ walk five miles to school every day, even in the winter.

And in school, the children don't have to think **(9)** _____. In math class, for example, we **(10)** _____ add, subtract, multiply, and divide, using our heads. Kids don't use their heads **(11)** _____; they use calculators.

Computers have taken control over our lives. In my day, we didn't **(12)** _____ have computers. We didn't even have electricity. My mother **(13)** _____ spend all day cooking in the kitchen. Nobody eats home-cooked food **(14)** _____. Food **(15)** _____ taste better. It's all chemicals and preservatives now.

And people don't talk to each other **(16)** _____. They're too busy to talk, too busy to eat, too busy to think . . . .

Life **(17)** _____ be simple, but it isn't **(18)** _____.

Exercise 4 *(Focus 4)*

Take your answers from Exercise 2 and write new sentences, adding *but not anymore,* if possible.

EXAMPLE: *I used to have long hair, but I don't anymore.*

_____

_____

_____

_____

_____

_____

_____

_____

_____

_____

Exercise 5 *(Focus 4)*

Go back to Exercise 3 and underline all of the negative forms that are used with *anymore.* The first one is "they <u>don't stay</u> together."

Exercise 6 (Focus 5)

Circle T if the statement is true, and F if it is false.

T F **1.** There used to be a country called the Soviet Union, but there isn't anymore.

T F **2.** There's still a country called Italy.

T F **3.** Thomas Jefferson used to be President of the United States, and he still is.

T F **4.** They still haven't found Atlantis.

T F **5.** Anthony and Cleopatra used to float down the Nile River, and they still do.

T F **6.** They used to speak German in Ireland, and they still do.

T F **7.** There used to be a wall separating East Germany from West Germany in Berlin, and there still is.

T F **8.** Alaska used to belong to Russia, but it doesn't anymore.

T F **9.** The Taj Mahal used to be in India, and it still is.

T F **10.** There didn't use to be a country named Uzbekistan, and there still isn't.

Exercise 7 (Focus 6)

Holly and Greta have been friends since high school. Greta just went to their 20-year high-school reunion, but Holly couldn't go. In the following dialogue, they are talking about their former classmates. Look at the pictures and complete the dialogue, using the correct form of the verb in parentheses and *still* or *anymore*.

Holly: Did you see Jim Jensen? He used to be so wild!

Greta: Yes, but he **(1)** _____ (be).
          He looks very conservative now.

Holly: Was he thin in high school? I don't remember.

Greta: Yes, and he **(2)** _____ (be).

Holly: **(3)** _____ (he, wear)
          glasses?

Greta: Yes, he does.

Holly: **(4)** _____ (he, play)
          the guitar?

Greta: Yes, he does, but now he plays classical guitar. He
          (5) _____ (play rock and roll).

Holly: Didn't he use to have long hair?

Greta: Yes, he did. But now he's bald. I also saw Jan Bissing at the reunion. Remember her? She used to be the most popular girl in school.

Holly: What does she look like now? **(6)** _____ (she, look) the same?

Greta: Yeah, except for her hair. She **(7)** _____ (have) long, brown hair. It's short and blonde. And she **(8)** _____ (be) cute! She **(9)** _____ (have) those big blue eyes and those thick eyelashes.

Holly: There was something different about her...didn't she always use to wear a hat?

Greta: Yes, and she **(10)** _____ (do).

Holly: Didn't she use to date George Weissler?

Greta: She **(11)** _____ (do)! They've been married for 18 years.

Exercise 8 *(Focus 7)*

Look at the information in the chart below and answer the questions, using *still, anymore,* or an **adverb of frequency.** Be careful with verb tenses.

	Before	**Now**
always	go dancing on weekends	stay home on weekends
often/ usually	go out to eat travel	cook dinner clean the house do the laundry
sometimes	read novels go to the beach	help kids with homework go to the beach go to baseball games
seldom/ hardly ever	cook clean	read novels go out to eat
never	stay home on weekends go to baseball games have children	go dancing travel

Carol used to be single. Last year she married George. George is divorced and has two children. The chart shows how Carol's life has changed.

1. Before she got married, how often did Carol use to go dancing?

   _____

2. Did Carol use to have children?

   _____

3. How often does Carol help the kids with their homework?

   _____

4. When she was single, what did Carol often use to do on her vacation?

   _____

5. How often did Carol use to cook and clean?

   _____

6. How often does Carol cook and clean now?

   _____

7. Does Carol still go dancing?

   _____

8. Does she still go to the beach?

   _____

9. How often does she go out to eat?

   _____

10. How often does she do the laundry?

   _____

UNIT 17

Past and Perfect and *Before* and *After*

Exercise 1 *(Focus 1)*

Read about Jerry, and then fill in the time line with brief phrases describing Jerry's life. Include only the underlined verbs. The first one has been done for you.

Jerry Zimmerman used to be a typical young man. Then five years ago, a car accident changed his life forever. The accident paralyzed him, and now he's in a wheelchair.

After the accident, Jerry was in the hospital for a long time. He had a lot of operations. He had never been in the hospital before, and he had never seen so many doctors: surgeons, anesthesiologists, neurologists... He had never felt so much pain; he was sure the physical therapists were experts in torture. He had to learn to get around in a wheelchair, too.

Before the accident, Jerry had played tennis and he had sailed. Now he's learning to play table tennis, and he still sails his boat on the lake. He also competes in races in his wheelchair. He had always had a dog, but after the accident, he needed a specially trained dog to help him around the house. Last year he got Bridget, a Black Labrador.

As for his love life, Jerry had been engaged to a girl named Debbie. He's still going to be married, but now he's engaged to Patty—his physical therapist.

Before accident	After accident	Now
1. _____	1. *Jerry was in the hospital.*	1. _____
2. _____	2. _____	2. _____
3. _____	3. _____	3. _____
4. _____	4. _____	4. _____
5. _____	5. _____	5. _____
6. _____		
7. _____		

Exercise 2 (Focus 2)

A reporter is interviewing Jerry (Exercise 1) for a feature story about the disabled. The reporter wants to know about Jerry's life before he was paralyzed. Using the words given below, write the reporter's questions and Jerry's answers. Use the **past perfect**.

E X A M P L E : your life / pretty normal?

Had your life been pretty normal?   *Yes, it had.*

1. How many times / you / be in the hospital / before the accident?

   _____

   _____

2. What sports / you / play / before the accident?

   _____

   _____

3. you / run in races?

   _____

4. Before Bridget, / you / have a dog?

   _____

5. you / be engaged to Patty?

   _____

Exercise 3 (Focus 2)

Combine the following pairs of statements to make one sentence, using the word in parentheses to connect them. Change one of the verbs into the **past perfect**.

E X A M P L E : Allen had a fight with his wife.

   He slept badly last night. (because)

   Allen slept badly last night because he had had a fight with his wife.

1. He slept late.

   Nobody set the alarm. (because)

   _____

2. Nobody did the laundry.

   Allen didn't have any clean underwear. (because)

   _____

   _____

3. Nobody went grocery shopping.
There wasn't any coffee. (because)

_____

_____

4. Allen forgot to go to the gas station.
There wasn't any gas in the car. (because)

_____

_____

5. He was very worried.
His boss warned him not to be late anymore. (because)

_____

_____

6. He didn't cash his paycheck, so he used a credit card.
He got to the gas station. (when)

_____

_____

7. He looked in the mirror and saw that he didn't comb his hair.
He was driving. (While)

_____

_____

8. Allen found that he left his wallet at the gas station.
He got to work. (As soon as)

_____

_____

9. He noticed there were no cars in the parking lot.
He realized that he forgot it was Saturday. (when)

_____

_____

Exercise 4 *(Focus 3)*

In each of the following sentences, write 1 above the action that occurred first, and 2 above the action that was second. If there are three verbs, write 3 above the third action. Then check (✔) the sentences where it is necessary to use the **past perfect** to indicate the order of events. The first one has been done for you.

1. __ Last night Mr. Wilson walked the dog and then let the cat out.

2. __ He locked the doors, turned off the lights, and went upstairs.

3. __ When he got upstairs, he realized that he had forgotten to take out the garbage.

4. __ He went back downstairs and took out the garbage.

5. __ When he went upstairs to brush his teeth, he heard a noise.

6. __ By the time Mr. Wilson got to the door, the noise had stopped.

7. __ He went back upstairs and heard the noise again. It sounded like someone crying.

8. __ He went back downstairs, and again, before he reached the door, the noise had stopped.

9. __ By that time, Mr. Wilson had gone up and down the stairs so many times that he was dizzy. He went to bed.

10. __ The next morning when Mr. Wilson went outside to get the newspaper, he saw what had caused the noise the night before.

11. __ He was surprised to see that the cat had had kittens!

Exercise 5 *(Focus 3)*

Answer the following questions about Mr. Wilson (Exercise 4) with complete sentences.

E X A M P L E : Did Mr. Wilson walk the dog last night?

Yes, he walked the dog.

1. Had Mr. Wilson let the cat out when he went upstairs?

   _____

2. What was he doing when he first heard the noise?

   _____

3. What did Mr. Wilson do when he heard the noise?

   _____

4. Why did he first go back downstairs?

   _____

5. Did Mr. Wilson hear the noise before or after he went upstairs?

_____

6. Why did he feel dizzy?

_____

7. What had Mr. Wilson done by the time he locked the doors and turned off the lights?

_____

8. By the time he went to bed, how many times had Mr. Wilson walked up the stairs?

_____

_____

9. What had caused the noise?

_____

_____

Exercise 6 *(Focus 4)*

For each space on the next page, choose the appropriate verb from the list and write in the correct verb tense (**simple past**, **past perfect**, **present perfect**, **simple present**, or **present progressive**). If there's a word in parentheses, include it in your answer. Some verbs are used more than once. The first one has been done for you.

be	have	teach
fall	learn	visit
fish	move	walk
get	see	wear
go	stay	write
grow	take	

Last winter Yarima Good _took_ a trip into the past. She _____ to visit her people, the Yanomama, in South America, one of the most primitive cultures on Earth.

Yarima _____ from the Stone Age to the 20th century six years ago. Before then, she _____ (never) clothes or _____ in shoes. Since then, she _____ to make light with a little plastic thing on the wall. She _____ (also) not to be afraid of mirrors or toilets or cars.

Anthropologist Kenneth Good first _____ South America in 1975. He _____ the first *nabuh*, or outsider, Yarima _____ (ever). She _____ a child then. Ken _____ with the Yanomama for twelve years. As a child, Yarima _____ with him in the river; then she _____ up. They _____ in love and _____ married.

Now Yarima _____ the stranger, the *nabuh*, living in a place where everything _____ different. She _____ three children, and because of them, _____ to live in this new world outside of New York City. For the Yanomama, the only counting system is one, two, and many, so Yarima's tutor _____ her to count. She _____, but it _____ (not) easy.

Ken Good _____ a book about his Amazon adventure, *Into the Heart*.

(Based on "Stone Age to Suburbs," by Nancy Shulins, Associated Press, *The Miami Herald*, January 3, 1992.)

UNIT 18

Quantity Classifiers with Food Items

Exercise 1 *(Focus 1)*

Mrs. Griffin sent her husband shopping, but the shopping list got torn. Can you help Mr. Griffin by completing the list? The first one has been done for you.

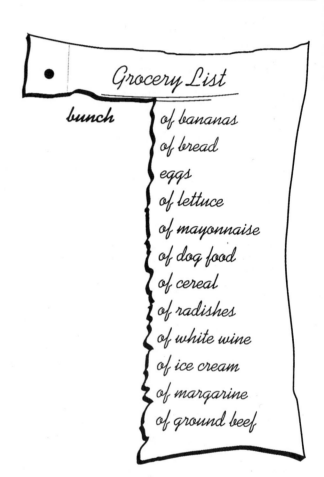

Grocery List

bunch of bananas
_____ of bread
_____ eggs
_____ of lettuce
_____ of mayonnaise
_____ of dog food
_____ of cereal
_____ of radishes
_____ of white wine
_____ of ice cream
_____ of margarine
_____ of ground beef

Exercise 2 *(Focus 1)*

GROUP

I went next door to borrow...

This is a game to test your memory. All players should sit in a circle. The first player begins by saying, "I went next door to borrow a can of anchovies" (or a bag of apples — any food that begins with the letter "A"). The second player repeats what the first player says, and then adds another item which begins with the letter "B": "I went next door to borrow a can of anchovies and a bunch of bananas." The third player must repeat what the first two players

114

have said and add another item which begins with "C": "I went next door to borrow a can of anchovies, a bunch of bananas, and a piece of cake," and so on until the whole alphabet has been completed.

Exercise 3 *(Focus 2)*

Unscramble the measure expressions for these recipes. The first one has been done for you as an example.

Avocado Freezer Ice Cream

(pusc)   2 *cups* of milk

(ucp)   ½ _____ of granulated sugar

(saoeonpt)   ¼ _____ of salt

                2 well-beaten eggs

(nitp)   1 _____ of heavy cream

(tsoaeonp)   1 _____ lemon extract

(puc)   1 _____ of sieved avocado

Combine milk, sugar, and salt; scald. Pour over eggs, stirring constantly. Add cream and lemon extract and cool.

Add avocado and mix thoroughly. Freeze in ice cream freezer. Makes about 1 quart.

Cheese Enchiladas

(zdnoe)   1 _____
                corn tortillas (12)

(tinp)   1 _____ enchilada sauce

(bsnaptoole)   1 _____
                onion, chopped

(nopud)   1 _____
                Cheddar cheese, shredded

(soenuc)   8 _____
                sour cream

For each enchilada, dip a tortilla into heated enchilada sauce. Put some onion, cheese, and sour cream on the tortilla and roll the tortilla around it. Pour the remaining sauce and any leftover cheese on top. Bake at 325° for 30 minutes.

Choose the <u>one</u> word or phrase that best completes the sentence.

1. Roy had a heart attack last year. Before then, he _____ about his health. His doctor told him to change his lifestyle, and gave him a diet and exercise plan.
   - (A) had never thought
   - (B) had thought never
   - (C) never had been thinking
   - (D) never had thought

2-3. He started to eat more fruits and vegetables and less fat. Instead of eating a _____ of chocolate when he wanted something sweet, Roy learned to eat an apple or a _____ of grapes.

   2. (A) box
      (B) bar
      (C) clove
      (D) tablet

   3. (A) bunch
      (B) dozen
      (C) leaf
      (D) scoop

4. He used to eat a lot of fast food and he _____ any fresh vegetables.
   - (A) ate seldom
   - (B) had eaten seldom
   - (C) seldom used to eat
   - (D) used to seldom eat

5. Before his heart attack, Roy _____ a lot of salt and fried food.
   - (A) did use to eat
   - (B) use to eat
   - (C) used to eat
   - (D) was use to eat

6-7. He _____, but now he buys _____ of frozen yogurt instead of ice cream.

   6. (A) doesn't eat dessert anymore
      (B) eats dessert anymore
      (C) eats dessert still
      (D) still eats dessert

   7. (A) bags
      (B) cups
      (C) jars
      (D) quarts

8. Roy quit smoking and drinking hard liquor. After he _____for about three months, he started to feel a lot better.
   - (A) had been quitting
   - (B) has quit
   - (C) had quit
   - (D) used to quit

9. After his doctor advised Roy to start an exercise program, he _____ to walk every morning before work.

    (A) began   (C) begun

    (B) begins   (D) had begun

10. It's been one year since Roy's heart attack, and he feels great. He _____ a cigarette anymore.

    (A) didn't want   (C) still wants

    (B) doesn't want   (D) wanted

Identify the one underlined word or phrase that must be changed in order for the sentence to be grammatically correct.

11. When I was a little boy, every Thanksgiving weekend my family and I were used to visit
     A   **B**   **C**   **D**
my grandparents on their farm.

12. We lived in the city, so it had been very special for us, especially me and my sister, to be
     A   **B**   **C**
in the country and to help Grandpa Bob with the animals and Grandma Flo with the
                 D
baking.

13. By the time we got to the farm on Wednesday night, Grandma had baked her world-
    A   **B**   **C**
famous homemade cinnamon bread and Grandpa had chose a turkey for Thanksgiving
                                        D
dinner.

14. Thursday morning we always used to get up early, toast a few slices of Flo's cinnamon
                A   **B**   **C**
bread for breakfast, and then go out to the garden to clean the best head of pumpkin
                                                D
for the pumpkin pie.

15. Then my sister and I used to play in the brightly colored autumn leaves; we had made
                    A   **B**
castles and mountains from the leaves, and then jumped and ran and laughed until Dad
                                  C
called us.
 D

16. The three of us helped Grandpa with the cows and the chickens, but mostly we played
             A   **B**
with the cats and dog; we children used to do seldom very much real work.
                           C   **D**

17. After we had played and worked so much, we were tired; my sister and I took a long
          A   **B**   **C**
nap while Mom and Dad had continued to help with all the work in the kitchen.
                         D

18. When it <u>was</u> finally time for Thanksgiving dinner, it <u>had always been</u> a feast: there was
        A   **B**

    a gigantic roasted turkey with stuffing, plates of vegetables from the garden, bowls of

    cranberries, <u>slices of</u> homemade bread with <u>pats of</u> fresh butter, and pieces of pumpkin
                    C   **D**

    pie for dessert.

19. Now I'm married, I have my own family, and I live in the city <u>still</u>; my grandparents
                                                              A

    <u>died</u> many years ago, so we <u>don't visit</u> the farm <u>anymore</u>.
     B   **C**   **D**

20. I <u>didn't use</u> to cook, but now that Grandma's not here, she <u>doesn't</u> bake <u>anymore</u> that
      A   **B**   **C**

    wonderful cinnamon bread, so <u>I've learned</u> to make it myself.
                                 D

UNIT

19

Articles

Exercise 1 *(Focus 1)*

Read the following story. For all the underlined nouns, write *D* above nouns with **definite articles** and *I* above nouns with **indefinite articles**.

Rigoberta Menchu is a young Guatemalan Indian <u>woman</u>. In 1993 she won the Nobel Peace <u>Prize</u> for her work for the <u>Indians</u> of Guatemala.

In the <u>book</u>, *I Rigoberta Menchu*, she tells her life story and about some <u>customs</u> and <u>ceremonies</u> of the Quiché Indians. She begins by telling about how as a young <u>girl</u> of eight, she helped her family by working on a coffee <u>plantation</u>. It was hard <u>work</u> to pick the coffee <u>beans</u> and weed the coffee <u>plants</u>.

Most of the <u>story</u> tells about how the <u>army</u> and the <u>government</u> tried to control the <u>Indians</u> by taking property and killing many Indians. Rigoberta's father, mother, and one of her brothers were killed by <u>soldiers</u>.

Rigoberta has tried to fight the <u>violence</u> with peace. She helped to start the <u>PUC</u> (a peasant unity <u>committee</u>), which has tried to oppose the <u>government</u> peacefully.

Exercise 2 *(Focus 2)*

Complete the following story with *a, an,* or *the* as appropriate. The first one has been done for you as an example.

A Fractured Fairy Tale

One morning Papa Bear, Mama Bear, and Baby Bear couldn't eat their porridge because it was too hot. So _the_ three bears went for _____ walk while their porridge cooled. While they were gone, Goldilocks came in. She saw _____ porridge cooling. First, she tried Papa's bowl, but _____ porridge was too hot. Next, she tried Mama's bowl, but _____ porridge was too cold. Then, she tried Baby Bear's porridge, and it was just right, so she ate it all up.

After that, Goldilocks was tired, so she looked for _____ place to rest. She found _____ bedrooms. She tried Papa's room, but _____ bed was too hard. Then, she tried Mama's bed, but it was too soft. Finally, she tried Baby's bed, and it was just right. She felt so comfortable that she fell asleep.

When _____ bears came home, they found _____ big surprise. Papa Bear looked at _____ spoon in his bowl and said, "Someone has been eating my porridge."

Mama looked at _____ spoon in her bowl and said, "Someone has been eating _____ porridge, all right."

When he looked at his bowl, Baby Bear began to cry. _____ bowl was empty.

When Mama went to her bedroom, she found _____ covers disturbed on her bed.

"Look, Papa, _____ beds are a mess."

"Yes," Papa agreed. "Someone has been sleeping in my bed too."

"Here she is!" shouted Baby Bear.

At the sound of _____ Bear's voice, Goldilocks jumped up and ran out.

However, the police caught her. She was arrested and charged with unlawful entry, stealing porridge, and bad manners. The judge sentenced her to three months at Miss Manners' School of Etiquette.

Exercise 3 (Focus 2)

Read over the exercise above. For each time the word _the_ is a correct answer, decide why it is used. If it is used because it is the second mention of the noun following it, write _S_ above it. If it is used because a related noun has been mentioned, write _R_ above it.

Exercise 4 (Focus 3)

Complete the following story with *a*, *an*, or *the* as appropriate. The first one has been done for you as an example.

Now it's time for our nightly weather report. This was *the* rainiest day ever for _____ first day of spring. It wasn't _____ best day for getting _____ good look at _____ sun, but _____ rain was needed. This has been _____ driest spring on record.

The plants really needed _____ rain. _____ high temperature was 65° today, and _____ low temperature was 40°. _____ three-day forecast calls for more rain. But don't worry, things will clear up for _____ weekend.

Exercise 5 (Focus 4)

Complete the following story with *a*, *an*, *the*, or *some* as appropriate. The first one has been done for you as an example.

On *a* cool fall day, _____ grasshopper was watching _____ ants put away _____ food that they had worked to collect all summer.

"Do you have any food you could share with _____ grasshopper?" he asked.

_____ ant stopped his work.

"What were you doing all summer?" he asked.

"I was singing _____ songs and practicing _____ new dances," answered _____ grasshopper.

"Songs and dances won't help you survive _____ long winter," said _____ ant. "You should have made _____ plan for _____ winter."

Exercise 6 *(Focus 5)*

Fill in the blanks in the story below with *the* or the zero (∅) article.

Newfoundland is one province of Canada which attracts _____ tourists of all ages.
Much of _____ province is on Newfoundland Island and separated from Canada's
mainland. _____ ferries and _____ airplanes bring _____ passengers from all over _____ world. _____ rugged coast of this island is full
of _____ natural beauty. _____ tourists marvel at _____ fjords and
_____ inlets in Gros Morne National Park. _____ nature is everywhere
on Newfoundland Island. _____ people watch for _____ birds such as:
_____ eagles, _____ seagulls, _____ cormorants, and _____
gillemots; or they look for _____ pilot whales. Yes, _____ life is beautiful on
Newfoundland Island.

Articles with Geographical and Institutional Terms

Exercise 1 *(Focus 1)*

Read the following description of Canada. Underline all the geographical names. On the next page, list the geographical names that don't take articles on the left and geographical names that do take articles on the right. The first one has been done for you as an example.

Canada

Canada is the northernmost country in North America. Canada is bordered by the United States on the south, the Arctic Ocean on the north, the Atlantic Ocean on the east, and the Pacific Ocean and Alaska on the west. Canada is divided into 10 provinces: Newfoundland, New Brunswick, Nova Scotia, Prince Edward Island, Quebec, Ontario, Manitoba, Saskatchewan, Alberta, British Columbia, and two territories: Yukon Territory and Northwest Territories. The two highest mountains in Canada are Mount Logan at 19,850 feet above sea level and Mount St. Elias at 18,008 feet above sea level. Canada's largest lakes are Lake Huron, Great Bear Lake, Lake Superior, and Great Slave Lake.

No Articles	Articles
1. *Canada*	1.
2.	2.
3.	3.
4.	4.
5.	
6.	
7.	
8.	
9.	
10.	
11.	
12.	
13.	
14.	
15.	
16.	
17.	
18.	
19.	
20.	
21.	
22.	
23.	
24.	

Exercise 2 *(Focus 1)*

Write a paragraph about the geography of your native country. Use an encyclopedia for help with specific facts, if necessary.

Exercise 3 *(Focus 2)*

Test your knowledge of world geography. Name a geographical location for each category which begins with the letter at the top of the column. Be sure to include articles for the places that require them.

	M	G	S
Rivers			
Deserts			
Cities			
Lakes			

	H	A	R
Islands and island chains			
Mountain chains or peaks			
Streets in your city			

	P	M	N
States or provinces			
Planets			
Oceans or seas			

Exercise 4 *(Focus 2)*

You can do the activity in exercise 3 as a competitive game. You need one person to serve as a timer. Each player lists the same three categories on a sheet of paper. The timer calls out four letters of the alphabet. Each player writes the letters at the top of the columns. Then each player fills in as many geographical names as possible for the categories. After five minutes, the timer calls "stop." The player with the most names with the correct article wins.

Exercise 5 *(Focus 3)*

In 1992, Hurricane Andrew destroyed more property than any other natural disaster in the United States. Not only did it destroy homes and businesses, but many public institutions were damaged too. Use the information from the chart to write sentences about the places that Hurricane Andrew damaged. Be sure to use the article *the* as appropriate.

Slightly Damaged	Damaged	Heavily Damaged
Colleges or Universities		
1. Barry University	2. Miami-Dade Community College (Wolfson Campus)	3. University of Miami
4. St. Thomas University		5. Florida International
		6. Miami-Dade Community College (Homestead Campus)
Parks		
7. Oleta River State Park	8. Morningside Park	9. Biscayne National Park
10. Greynolds Park		11. Everglades National Park
		12. Fairchild Tropical Gardens
Buildings and Attractions		
13. Freedom Tower	14. Micasooki Indian Reservation	15. Deering Estate
16. Port of Miami		17. Zoo

1. *Barry University was slightly damaged by Hurricane Andrew.* _____

2. _____

3. _____

4. _____

5. _____

6. _____

7. _____

8. _____

9. _____

10. _____

11. _____

12. _____

13. _____

14. _____

15. _____

16. _____

17. _____

Indirect Objects with *For*

Exercise 1 *(Focus 1)*

Unscramble the following sentences. Be careful with word order (i.e., put the **direct object** before the **indirect object**). The first one has been done for you as an example.

1. door / for / He / her / opened / the

   He opened the door for her.

2. him / note / passed / She / the / to

   _____

3. cut / dad /for / grass / her / She / the

   _____

4. before / children / Christmas / letters / Many / Santa Claus / to /write

   _____

5. a / bought / Diana / for / puppy / We

   _____

Puppy

6. a / for / her / Her / made / sandwich / sister

   _____

7. hand / homework / in / usually / Students / teacher / the / their / to

   _____

8. children / often / Parents / read / stories / their / to

   _____

9. braided / for / hair / her / her / Jack

   _____

BRAID

10. Barbara / handed / mailman / package / The / the / to

_____

Exercise 2 *(Focus 2)*

Look at the picture and fill in the blank with *to* or *for*. Then number the picture 1, for what happened first, or 2, for what happened second.

1. When she finished translating the letter _____ him, she gave it _____ him.

2. The mechanic sold a tire _____ Mrs. Captain. Then she had a flat tire, and someone changed it _____ her.

3. Kelly threw the ball _____ Bobby, and he caught it. But later, Bobby fell, and Kelly had to catch the ball _____ him.

4. In art class, Andy drew a picture _____ his mother. He gave it _____ her when he got home.

5. Lindsey pulled the wagon _____ Jonathan. Then she pulled the wagon _____ him because he wasn't strong enough.

6. Ann couldn't reach the shelf, so she asked Cheryl to get the jar _____ her. Cheryl got the jar and handed it _____ Ann.

7. Mike left a message _____ Corey. As soon as she got back to the office, Larry gave it _____ her.

8. Luke couldn't reach the potatoes, so Aunt Betty passed the plate _____ him. After Uncle John served the potatoes, he passed the plate back _____ Luke.

9. Karen asked Brian to bring the baby _____ her. She got tired, so Brian carried the baby _____ her.

10. Mark wrote a love letter _____ his sweetheart, and then he bought a present _____ her.

Exercise 3 *(Focus 2)*

Work with a partner and take turns asking and answering questions about the pictures on the following pages.

EXAMPLE: Student 1: *What did she do for him?*

Student 2: *She translated a letter for him.*

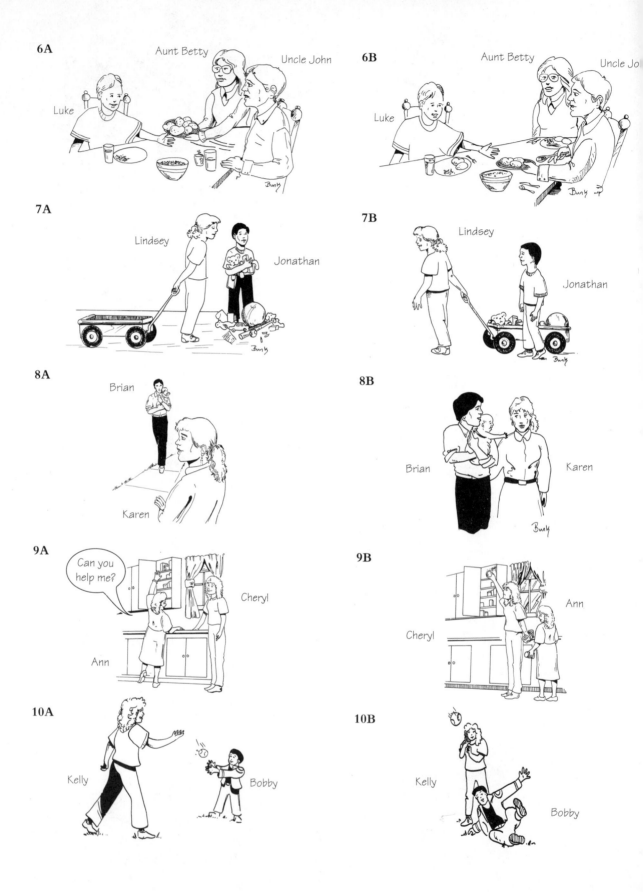

Exercise 4 (Focus 4)

Rewrite each of the following sentences. Omit *for* and put the **indirect object** in its proper place.

E X A M P L E :   Mom always cooks my favorite foods for me.
Mom always cooks me my favorite foods.

1. Gin sewed a silk tie for her husband.

   _____

2. Justin built a dog house for the dog.

   _____

3. Larry baked an apple pie for Paula.

   _____

4. Edwin gets toys for his nephews.

   _____

5. Slaven bakes bread for his family.

   _____

6. Nelly will save a place in line for you.

   _____

7. Edith knit that beautiful green sweater for Van Lee.

   _____

8. Canada saved millions of dollars for the taxpayers.

   _____

9. Carlos can stop and buy the milk for us.

   _____

10. Patricio made a new picture frame for Maria.

    _____

11. Jeff bought a new computer game for Erik.

    _____

Exercise 5 (Focus 3 & 4)

Answer the following questions, using the cues from the list. Use *for* when you think it is more important to emphasize *who* benefits from the action; omit *for* when you think it is best to emphasize *what* they receive. The first two have been done for you as examples.

Erin and Mark Jennings just had a new baby boy, Daniel. After Daniel was born, many of their friends and family helped them out and gave them gifts. Erin kept a list of all these things so she could write thank-you notes.

Gave Gifts

Doug and Carol bought diapers
Karen knit a baby blanket
Rebecca sewed three bibs
Jackie bought a stroller
Marilyn brought me flowers
Tim got a crib

Helped Out

Mom cooked dinner for Mark
Dan baked a cake for me
Dennis built a storage shelf for the baby
Janet made soup for us
Ray built a changing table

1. Who did Tim get the crib for?

   Tim got the crib for the baby.

2. What did Ray build?

   Ray built a changing table.

3. What did Karen knit?

4. Who did Doug and Carol buy diapers for?

5. What did Janet make?

6. Who did Rebecca sew bibs for?

7. What did Doug and Carol buy?

8. What did Dennis build?

9. What did Rebecca sew?

10. Who did Dan bake a cake for?

11. What did Marilyn buy?

12. Who did Jackie buy the stroller for?

13. Who did Karen knit the blanket for?

_____

14. What did Erin's mom do?

_____

15. Who did Janet make soup for?

_____

Exercise 6 *(Focus 5)*

Rewrite the following story. Omit *for* if possible. The first sentence has been done for you as an example.

On my husband's birthday, I always prepare a special meal for him. First, I bake homemade bread for him. Then I cook his favorite meal, lasagne, for him. I also buy the best wine for him.

Last year, I had a problem, though. We were staying in a vacation cabin and I had a stove, but I didn't have an oven. My son and daughter solved the problem for me. They suggested that I make spaghetti for him instead of lasagne.

They went to the little market near the cabin for me and bought noodles, tomato sauce, meat, and spices for me. Then they had to carry the groceries all the way back to the cabin for me.

When I asked my daughter to open the noodles for me, they spilled all over. My son cleaned up the noodles for her. He repaired the damage for her.

On my husband's birthday, I always prepare him a special meal. _____

_____

_____

_____

_____

_____

_____

_____

_____

_____

_____

_____

Identify the one underlined word or phrase that must be changed in order for the sentence to be grammatically correct.

1. The Philippines are a group of islands located in the South Pacific, north of the Indonesia.
   A   B   C   D

2. I sewed my daughter a dress for her birthday. She loved it because a dress was silk.
             A   B   C   D

3. It was hard to decide which college to apply to in the California: the University
                                                  A   B
   of California or Stanford.
       C   D

4. Grand Canyon is one of the most popular of all the National Parks in North America.
       A   B   C   D

5. I carried for my teacher the books she needed for class.
           A   B   C D

6. On the Sundays, my mom always cooks a big dinner for the whole family.
       A   B   C   D

7. The Great Lakes, which make up part of the border between Canada and the United States,
    A   B   C
   consist of the Lake Ontario, Lake Erie, Lake Huron, Lake Michigan, and Lake Superior.
          D

8. My job is to prepare the party a toss salad. The salad must be fresh.
       A   B   C   D

9. A astronaut explained the problems of space exploration to us.
    A   B   C   D

10. At the southern tip of Vancouver island is the city of the Victoria.
       A   B   C   D

11. I had the problems with the homework. Did you understand the solution for number 5?
        A   B   C   D

12. Ben tried to to repair me my car, but the car was too old. We had to sell it to
            A   B
    the junk yard and buy a new one.
       C   D

13. I've got an flat tire on my car. Could you fix it for me?
        A   B   C   D

14. The Biology includes the study of plants and animals.
       A   B   C   D

15. The place I would like to visit is the Andes Mountains in the South America.
       A   B   C   D

16. I can make sushi for you if you want to taste some typical food from the Japan.
    A   B   C   D

Choose the <u>one</u> word or phrase that best completes the sentence.

17. My husband still buys _____.
    (A) flowers to me   (C) for me flowers
    (B) me flowers   (D) to me flowers

18. I like fruit. I had _____ banana and _____ apple for lunch.
    (A) the . . . the   (C) an . . . a
    (B) a . . . a   (D) a . . . an

19. One of the most famous mountains in North America is _____, a volcano which exploded in 1980.
    (A) Mt. St. Helens   (C) a Mt. St. Helens
    (B) the Mt. St. Helens   (D) an Mt. St. Helens

20. What did he buy you? He bought _____.
    (A) a necklace for me   (C) a necklace to me
    (B) me a necklace   (D) for me a necklace

21. The highest building in the world is _____, which is located in _____.
    (A) Sears Tower . . . Chicago   (C) the Sears Tower . . . the Chicago
    (B) the Sears Tower . . . Chicago   (D) Sears Tower . . . the Chicago

22. That is _____ silliest thing you have ever said. It never snows in Miami.
    (A) the   (C) an
    (B) a   (D) some

23. I like the theater. I would like to see _____ more plays.
    (A) the   (C) an
    (B) a   (D) some

24. The Rio Grande makes up the border between _____.
    (A) the Mexico and the Texas   (C) Mexico and the Texas
    (B) the Mexico and Texas   (D) Mexico and Texas

25. The fiftieth state in _____.
    (A) the U.S. is the Hawaii   (C) U.S. is the Hawaii
    (B) the U.S. is Hawaii   (D) U.S. is Hawaii

26. _____ SUNY, is a large university system in New York.

    (A) The State University of New York, or the

    (B) The State University of New York, or

    (C) State University of New York, or the

    (D) State University of New York, or

27. Who did Angela prepare the income taxes for? _____.

    (A) Angela prepared them for Joseph

    (B) Angela prepared Joseph the income taxes

    (C) Angela prepared the income taxes to Joseph

    (D) Angela prepared him the income taxes

28. _____ is the closest planet to _____.

    (A) The mars . . . the earth

    (B) Mars . . . an earth

    (C) Mars . . . the earth

    (D) A Mars . . . earth

29. She saved _____ on the bus.

    (A) the place for me

    (B) me a place

    (C) for me the place

    (D) for me a place

30. Stevie got _____ because she was thirsty.

    (A) a soda to mom

    (B) for mom the soda

    (C) a soda for mom

    (D) the mom for the soda

The Passive

Exercise 1 (Focus 1)

Read the following report from a local newspaper describing a car accident. As the editor, you have to decide which is more appropriate, active or passive voice, and put a check (✔) next to it. The first one has been done for you.

1. ___ A car accident injured a seven-year-old boy on Wednesday.
   ✔ A seven-year-old boy was injured in a car accident on Wednesday.

2. ___ A bus was hit by the boy's father, Donald Derby, at the intersection of 1st Avenue and Spencer Street.
   ___ The boy's father, Donald Derby, hit a bus at the intersection of 1st Avenue and Spencer Street.

3. ___ A stop sign had been run by Derby.
   ___ Derby had run a stop sign.

4. ___ The boy was thrown through the car window.
   ___ The force of the accident threw the boy through the car window.

5. ___ Derby's daughter, Debbie, age three, was also in the car, but the accident did not hurt her.
   ___ Derby's daughter, Debbie, age three, was also in the car, but was not hurt.

6. ___ An ambulance took the father to St. Christopher Hospital.
   ___ The father was taken to St. Christopher Hospital.

7. ___ The accident also injured the driver of the bus, Joe Barta.
   ___ The driver of the bus, Joe Barta, was also injured.

8. ___ An ambulance took him to Cedars Hospital, where doctors treated him.
   ___ He was taken to Cedars Hospital, where he was treated.

9. ___ Seat belts were not being worn by the Derbys.
   ___ The Derbys were not wearing seat belts.

10. ___ Derby will be charged with running a stop sign and driving without a license.
    ___ The police will charge Derby with running a stop sign and driving without a license.

Exercise 2 *(Focus 2)*

Complete the following letter, using the appropriate form of the passive voice in the **simple past**, **past perfect**, **present perfect**, or **future**.

Dear Julie,

The last time I wrote to you my life was very different. Do you remember that Charlie and I were thinking about leaving the city and moving far away? Well, we did it!

The decision to build our house in the North Woods of Canada _____ (make) three years ago. The lumber _____ (buy) and _____ (move) by truck over miles of bad road. The plans for the house _____ (draw up) on our dining room table. I was in charge of the work, but my contribution _____ (limit) to giving orders. Most of the work was done by professionals, although a lot of the house _____ (design) by Charlie. It's fabulous!

The house _____ (build) out of native Canadian pine in a large and beautiful field. The field _____ (cover) with summer flowers when we arrived. I'm sorry to say that the flowers _____ (cut) to make room for the house. Our puppy, Caesar, was delighted with his small dog house which _____ (build) in the back yard. While we were all working on the house, we _____ (visit) every day by some of the wild animals of northern Canada. We gave them names of Walt Disney characters. The deer

_____ (name) Bambi, the rabbit _____ (call) Thumper, and a small grey wolf (nickname) Goofy. The skunk in our front yard _____ (name) Flower. A fence _____ (build) to surround our two dozen acres of land. The house _____ (finish) in four months, before the autumn frost, but the inside _____ (not + paint) until the following spring.

Our furniture _____ (send) from the city, and we _____ (move) in by Halloween. But the only trick-or-treaters that _____ (see) that year were two raccoons, a woodchuck, and a fox.

That was three years ago. Since then we have decided to stay. Our apartment in the city _____ (sell), our employ- ers _____ (notify) that we're not returning to work (even though Charlie and I _____ [just + promote] when we decided to move), and all our friends _____ (tell). Soon Charlie and I _____ (both + employ) by different companies, but we _____ (allow) to stay here at home and work at the computer.

I thought that it was going to be difficult for the children to adjust, but Jonathan, Lind- sey, and Alex _____ (not + bother) at all by the change. They have made new friends, and they love playing outside every day. I love it because there's no traf- fic, polluted air, noise, or crime.

Well, Julie, I have to go. You're welcome to come up for a visit any time.

Love,

Nancy

Exercise 3 *(Focus 3)*

Decide if the *by* + agent phrase is necessary in all of the following. Cross out the *by* phrases that you think are unnecessary.

It's that time of year again. Every night, sea turtles are coming out of the water and up on the beach to lay their eggs. As soon as the turtles lay their eggs, the nests are covered with sand by the turtles, and then they go back into the sea. One of nature's mysteries, they return to the same place every year.

Early every morning before sunrise, marine biologists and volunteers go up and down the beach, looking for new nests. The nests are moved by them to a safer, darker area. The reason for this is that baby sea turtles are attracted by bright light. If there's a building with bright lights on the beach, the babies will go toward the building, instead of going toward the ocean, where they should be going. After the nests are moved by the people, the chances that the turtles will survive are increased by the people.

People can see a sea turtle by participating in a turtle watch between May and August. A turtle watch is held every night by The Department of Natural Resources. Reservations are required by them.

The sea turtle is protected by state and federal laws. People are being warned by officials to stay away from sea-turtle nests. If a person is caught by someone taking or bothering a sea turtle, its eggs, or its nest, that person will be fined $20,000 by the government, and he or she could spend a year in prison. There's a Sea Turtle Hot Line that people should call if a baby turtle is seen by them going away from the ocean.

(Based on "Sea Turtles Hit Beaches in Broward," by Alan Topelson, *The Miami Herald*, May 1, 1993.)

Get-Passive

Exercise 1 *(Focus 1)*

Complete the following story with the *be*-passive or the *get*-passive and the past participle of the verb. The first one has been done for you as an example.

A Weird Wedding

Bea Prepared and Larry Lucky got married last week. Some unexpected events happened during Bea and Larry's wedding and honeymoon.

First, one week before the wedding the minister *got transferred* (transfer) to a new church, so they had to find a replacement at the last minute. After that Larry _____ (lay off) unexpectedly. Then, on the night before the wedding Bea _____ (sick) from the fish she _____ (serve) for dinner.

On the day of the wedding, the flowers _____ (not deliver) because the florist _____ (lost) on the way to the church. During the ceremony, the organist _____ (confuse) and played the funeral march instead of the wedding march. Also, the bride's dress _____ (tear) when the groom accidentally stepped on it. Then, the ceremony _____ (interrupt) when a mouse came running through the church. The scared bridesmaids began to scream.

The reception was supposed to be held outdoors, but it started to rain and everyone _____ (wet). Bea and Larry went to Las Vegas for their honeymoon, but their luggage _____ (leave) at the airport.

Then Larry's wallet _____ (steal). Not everything went badly, though. In Las Vegas they got lucky and won a million dollars. Finally, they _____ (reward) for all their troubles.

Exercise 2 *(Focus 2)*

Use the following police reports as cues to write the conversations using the *get*-passive. The first one has been done for you as an example.

Crime Reports

1. Officers forced open the door of a Westwood home and confiscated two pounds of marijuana. The homeowner and another resident were charged with growing marijuana.

    Leigh: *Did you hear what happened in Westwood last night?*

    Ralph: *No. What?*

    Leigh: *The police made an arrest. Two pounds of marijuana got confiscated and two people got charged with growing marijuana.*

2. Eggs were thrown at a 1993 Lexus parked near the beach.

    Brian: _____

    Steve: _____

    Brian: _____

3. A camcorder and jewelry were stolen from a house in the Fallen Pines neighborhood.

    Judy: _____

    Les: _____

    Judy: _____

4. A golf cart was stolen from the tenth hole of the country club last week. The golfers had just come back from the club house when they noticed the cart was missing.

    Rita: _____

    Enrique: _____

    Rita: _____

146

5. Tools were stolen from a Power and Light Company storage truck. The burglars cut through a padlock.

Jorge: _____

Cecilia: _____

Jorge: _____

6. Burger King was robbed by two men on Saturday night.

Primrose: _____

Jossy: _____

Primrose: _____

7. A window was forced open and an apartment was ransacked. Nothing was stolen.

Anthony: _____

Eddie: _____

Anthony: _____

8. Three men were caught prowling at 3:20 A.M. in back of the Cool Condos.

Alexander: _____

Yana: _____

Alexander: _____

9. A camera and a set of binoculars were stolen from the Marco Polo Resort.

Victoria: _____

Angelica: _____

Victoria: _____

10. A bicycle was taken from a storage shed behind a home on 90th Street. The owner said she wasn't sure when the bike had been stolen.

Laura: _____

Ina: _____

Laura: _____

11. Plastic pink flamingos had been reported missing from several yards over the past two weeks. The police recovered them Saturday. The flamingos were found standing in the mayor's yard this morning.

Elvis: _____

Pricilla: _____

Elvis: _____

Exercise 3 (Focus 2)

PAIR

Work with a partner. Act out the dialogues based on the crime reports.

Exercise 4 (Focus 3)

Use the cues at the left to make sentences with the *get*-passive. The sentences at the top of each exercise will help you decide which tense to use.

Linda is a very busy working mother, but no matter how much work she does she always gets her housework done too.

1. clean/house _____
2. cook/meals _____
3. do/dishes _____

At this time many things are being done to improve our city. For example:

4. destroy/crack houses _____
5. renovate/historic buildings _____
6. build/low income housing _____

Every year our college does general repairs. These are some things that were done last year.

7. paint/halls _____
8. plant/trees _____
9. remodel/language lab _____

My friends and I were invited to a wedding. However, my friends arrived late. Tell what was going on at the reception when each friend arrived.

When _____ arrived,

10. Richard—seat for dinner/people _____
11. Lisa—serve/dinner _____
12. Angelica—cut/cake _____

In 1992, there were riots in Los Angeles over the verdict in the Rodney King trial. The National Guard was called in. However, by the time the National Guard arrived, a lot of damage had already been done.

By the time the National Guard arrived,

13. burn/buildings _____
14. loot/stores _____

Many companies are trying to figure out how they are going to deal with the recession. Some companies have decided that several changes will be made for next year. What changes will be made?

15. cut/salaries _____

16. lay off/employees _____

17. not hire/new employees _____

Exercise 5 *(Focus 4)*

Where possible, rewrite the underlined verbs with *get*-passives.

EXAMPLE: <u>Was</u> the work <u>done</u>?
Did the work get done?

1. The work <u>was finished</u> by the time I arrived.

   _____

2. You can buy your cola now—the machine <u>has been refilled</u>.

   _____

3. His true identity <u>was unknown</u>.

   _____

4. <u>Was</u> the house <u>damaged</u> in the the storm?

   _____

5. The house <u>was damaged</u>, but now it is <u>being repaired</u>.

   _____

6. The basis of the economic problem <u>was understood</u>, but the solution was difficult.

   _____

7. You'll have to wait—your uniform <u>hasn't been washed</u> yet.

   _____

8. She <u>was seen</u> at the party last night.

   _____

9. The dessert <u>will be frozen</u> in time for dinner.

   _____

10. The flat tire <u>will be fixed</u> so we can get to the meeting on time.

   _____

UNIT

24

Modals of Probability and Possibility

Exercise 1 *(Focus 1)*

You have found a purse containing the following items. Write the best answer in each space to complete the statements about the owner of the purse.

1. some makeup and nail polish

   The owner of the purse _____ a woman.

       could be   is   may be

2. a comb with gray hairs

   She _____ an older woman.

       could be   might be   must be

3. a government employee ID card

   She _____ for the government.

       could work   may work   must work

4-5. a lot of keys and computer disks

   She _____ a secretary.

       could be   is   must be

   She _____ a computer.

       doesn't use   must use   uses

6. pictures of children

   The children _____ her grandchildren, or they _____ her nieces and nephews.

       are   could be   might be

7. a glass case

   She _____ wear glasses, but the case _____ be for sunglasses.

       could   is   must

150

8. a bank statement showing a balance of $0.00

She _____ any money in the bank, but she

_____ another account.

could have   doesn't have   must have

9. an Irish passport full of stamps

She _____ be American. She _____

travel a lot.

might   must   must not

10. a small handgun

She _____ work for the police. She

_____ be a spy.

could   might   must

Exercise 2 *(Focus 2)*

Complete the following dialogues, using the correct form of *could, may, might,* or *must* with the verb in parentheses. Be careful—some of them are negative.

EXAMPLE: A: Lee hasn't smiled all day.

B: He <u>*must be*</u> in a bad mood. (be)

1. A: Every time I see Gigi, she's eating a candy bar.

B: She _____ chocolate. (like)

2. A: Julia has just finished working a 16-hour shift at the hospital.

B: She _____ tired. (be)

3. A: Are Jim and Marcia going to the party on Saturday?

B: I'm not sure. They _____ about the party. (know) Did you

tell them about it?

4. A: Our new neighbor wears a dark blue uniform to work.

B: He _____ a mailman, or he _____ a

police officer. (be)

5. A: When planning a party, remember to think of all your guests. Make sure to serve

dishes that don't include meat, especially pork.

B: Why? Because of guests who are vegetarians?

A: Yes. Some of them _____ meat. (eat)

6. A: Don't ignore chest pain.

B: Why?

A: You _____ heart disease. (have)

7. A: What's that game they're playing?

B: I don't know. It _____ rugby, or it

_____ lacrosse. (be)

8. A: Is Nancy single?

B: I don't know, but she wears a ring, and she's always talking about a man named Tim.

A: She _____ married. (be)

9. A: Look at that man! He's pushing all the peas to the side of his plate.

B: He _____ peas. (like)

10. A: That customs official is screaming at that lady, and she looks totally confused.

B: She _____ English. (understand)

Exercise 3 (Focus 3)

Complete the following dialogue, using *could, may, might,* or *must,* and the verb in parentheses. Be careful—some are in the present and others are in the past.

Gladys and her husband, Norman, are talking about their neighbors. Gladys is convinced that they are terrible people, but Norman isn't so sure. He thinks that Gladys is being a nosy neighbor and jumping to conclusions.

Gladys: Have you seen the car that the Riccios are driving? It's a Mercedes Benz! They don't make enough money to afford that car. They _____ (be) drug dealers.

Norman: Oh, Gladys. Mind your own business. They _____ (inherit) the money, or they _____ (win) the car in a contest. We don't know!

Gladys: And did you see their recycling last week? There _____ (be) a dozen wine bottles. They _____ (be) alcoholics.

Norman: Oh, Gladys. Mind your own business. Kathy and Tim _____ (have) a party, or they _____ (invite) friends over for dinner.

152

Gladys: Oh, yeah? Well, two weeks ago I saw their car parked in front of St. Jude's. Kathy _____ (go) to one of those AA (Alcoholics Anonymous) meetings that they hold there.

Norman: Gladys, you don't know that for sure. She _____ (be) at a store near the church. Mind your own business.

Gladys: Norman... Have you seen their little boy lately? He has cuts and bruises all over his body. Tim _____ (get) drunk and hit him. That's child abuse.

Norman: Gladys, the boy _____ (fall) off his bike. You know how kids are. Mind your own business.

Gladys: Norman...

Norman: Gladys, you _____ (be) crazy. You haven't even met those people!

Gladys: Norman, you _____ (be) right.

Exercise 4 (Focus 3 and 4)

Choose the best answer and write it in the space.

1. A: What are you going to do this weekend?

   B: My brother has tickets to the baseball game, so I _____ with him. My favorite team is playing.

       could go   'll probably go   must go

2. A: What are you going to do on your vacation?

   B: I'm not sure. We _____ a trip to Kenya and go on a safari.

       'll probably take   may take   must take

3. A: Do you have plans for tonight?

   B: Not really. I _____ just stay home and watch TV, as usual.

       could   'll probably   must

4. A: I wonder why Mike is wearing that bandage around his wrist.

   B: I don't know. He _____ it.

       might hurt   must have hurt   must hurt

5. A: Where are my keys?

B: You _____ them in the kitchen.

    may left   might have left   must leave

6. A: I haven't been feeling well lately, especially in the morning.

B: Really? You _____ pregnant. Maybe you've got morning sickness.

    could be   'll probably be   must be

7. A: Have you seen Lourdes?

B: Yes, and judging from the size of her stomach, she _____ at least seven months pregnant.

    could have been   'll probably be   must be

8. A: Are you going to visit your family this year?

B: I don't know. It depends on the airfares. I _____.

    could be   may be   might

9. A: What grade do you think you'll get in this class?

B: So far I have a pretty good average, and I've been studying a lot this semester.

    I _____ a B.

    could get   'll probably get   must get

10. A: Her hair always looks so stiff and thick.

B: I know. It looks so unnatural.

A: She _____ a wig.

    'll probably wear   might wear   must wear

Choose the <u>one</u> word or phrase that best completes the sentence.

1. Tortillas, the bread of Mexico, _____ with ground corn, water, and lime.
   - (A) are being made
   - (B) are made
   - (C) get made
   - (D) make

2. Many Mexicans buy tortillas at their local *tortillería*, where they are produced _____ machine.
   - (A) a
   - (B) by
   - (C) in
   - (D) with

3. Others, who _____ buy them, prefer to make their own.
   - (A) are
   - (B) could
   - (C) 'll probably
   - (D) must

4. Many women _____ the dough, or *masa*, between their hands and flatten it into a thin, round, pancake-like shape.
   - (A) are taken
   - (B) are taking
   - (C) have been taken
   - (D) take

5. The tortilla _____ in Mexico for centuries, since the days of the Aztecs.
   - (A) are eaten
   - (B) has been eating
   - (C) has been eaten
   - (D) is eating

6. A 28-year-old woman _____ to become the next princess. The prince made his decision after consulting his list of more than 100 candidates.
   - (A) chooses
   - (B) has been chosen
   - (C) is being chosen
   - (D) is choosing

7. At first, she didn't want to be on the "princess list." People said that she _____ a boyfriend.
   - (A) might have
   - (B) must have
   - (C) must have had
   - (D) was having

8. But the prince started calling her on the telephone every day. He _____ very convincing, because she changed her mind.
   - (A) may be
   - (B) might have been
   - (C) must have been
   - (D) was being

9. The future princess, a very independent and well-educated woman, _____ the very conservative role of princess.
   - (A) can changed
   - (B) change
   - (C) has been changed
   - (D) may change

10. A former diplomat, she speaks five languages and _____ in four countries.
    (A) educated
    (B) is educated
    (C) has educated
    (D) was educated

Identify the <u>one</u> underlined word or phrase that must be changed in order for the sentence to be grammatically correct.

11. Two tourists <u>were</u> <u>being</u> robbed <u>while</u> they <u>were</u> checking into the Sandy Shores Hotel.
               A   **B**   **C**   **D**

12. Police say that the couple <u>had</u> <u>been</u> left their bags unattended, and <u>when</u> they looked,
                         A   **B**   **C**
    the bags <u>had</u> disappeared.
          D

13. Police also say the bags <u>will</u> <u>have been</u> stolen <u>by</u> the same criminals who <u>have been</u>
                     A   **B**   **C**   **D**
    attacking foreign tourists in the area.

14. They <u>think</u> that it <u>can</u> be an employee of one of the hotels, or it <u>might</u> be someone
         A   **B**   **C**
    who <u>is</u> dressed like a tourist.
        D

15. Every year tourists around the world <u>get</u> <u>robbed</u> like this, because they become careless;
                               A **B**
    they <u>shouldn't</u> take their eyes off their luggage, or something like this <u>must</u> occur.
        C   **D**

16. South Dakota is <u>knowing</u> <u>for</u> Mount Rushmore, where the enormous heads of four
                   A   **B**
    U.S. presidents <u>are</u> <u>carved</u> in the side of a mountain.
              C   **D**

17. Kirczak Ziolkowski, who <u>was</u> <u>died</u> in 1982, <u>helped</u> carve Mt. Rushmore, and then he
                     A **B**   **C**
    bought a nearby mountain and <u>began to</u> carve a gigantic replica of the Sioux Chief
                              D
    Crazy Horse.

18. Ziolkowski's widow, Ruth, said that the sculpture was her husband's dream and that a
    strange relationship <u>had existed</u> between him and Crazy Horse: he <u>was</u> <u>borned</u> on the
                    A   **B**   **C**
    same day that Crazy Horse <u>died</u>, but 31 years later.
                       D

19. Ruth <u>says</u> that now that her husband is <u>dead</u>, his spirit <u>can</u> be with Crazy Horse's, and
          A   **B**   **C**
    they're <u>probably watching</u> the construction from heaven.
            D

20. The Ziolkowski family <u>has continued</u> to work on the huge project, and they say that
                       A
    it will <u>could</u> be many years before the sculpture is <u>finished</u>—their great grandchildren
          B   **C**
    <u>might</u> see a completed Crazy Horse.
     D

UNIT
25

Noun Complements

Exercise 1 *(Focus 1)*

Using the expressions from the list and your own ideas, complete the following sentences with *that*-clauses.

E X A M P L E : *I think that education and health care* should be free.

I believe that	It is a fact that
My teacher thinks that	It is my opinion that
It is possible that	It is true that
I think that	My parents think that

1. _____ should be banned. (*banned* = prohibited)

2. _____ the sun rises
   _____.

3. _____ people should be required to have a
   license to _____.

4. _____ it ought to be a crime to
   _____.

5. _____ people are basically
   _____.

6. _____ take advantage of
   _____.

7. _____ North Americans are
   _____.

8. _____ people from my native country are
   _____.

9. _____ life in North America is
   _____.

10. _____ life in my native country is

_____.

11. _____ the world is round.

Exercise 2 (Focus 2)

Look at your answers to Exercise 1. Without changing the meaning, rewrite only the sentences that you wrote with *think* and *believe*, using the negative form.

E X A M P L E : *I don't think that people should have to pay for education and health care.*

_____

_____

_____

_____

_____

_____

_____

_____

_____

Exercise 3 (Focus 3)

Using the words below, write sentences for the politician. The conversation on the left is between the politician and her husband at the breakfast table. The sentences on the right are part of a speech that she's giving. Remember that *that* is often omitted in informal speech.

BREAKFAST TABLE

Husband: What's your speech about today?

Politician: Our government's immigration policy.

I / not think / it / be / fair

POLITICAL SPEECH

I / not believe / our immigration policy / be / fair

Husband: What do you mean?

Politician: We welcome some people with open arms, and others we send back to their countries.

158

I / know / this / happen

I / realize / our government / send / some people back to their countries

I / think / it / be / wrong

It / be / my opinion / this / be / wrong

I / think / it / be / a racist policy

I / be / certain / it / be / a racist policy

Husband: But honey, immigration is a big problem. There are just too many people entering this country illegally. They take jobs away from our own taxpaying citizens.

Politician: I / doubt / this / happen

It / be / unlikely / immigrants / take jobs away from our citizens

I / believe / immigrants / do work that our citizens refuse to do

I / be / convinced / immigrants / do work that our citizens refuse to do

Phrasal Verbs

Exercise 1 *(Focus 1)*

Read the story. Then write the underlined **phrasal verbs** next to their meanings in the space below. Number 12 has been done for you as an example.

My teacher gave me the assignment to <u>find out</u> as much as I could about burial customs around the world and write a report about it. I <u>put off</u> doing my research for one week. When I couldn't wait any longer, I decided I had better go to the library and <u>look up</u> some information.

On the way to the library, I <u>ran into</u> my friend Brittany. She invited me to <u>go over</u> to her house. When I explained what I had to do, she offered to <u>help</u> me <u>out</u>.

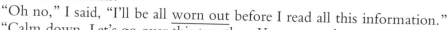

At the library, we found hundreds of books about burial customs.

"Oh no," I said, "I'll be all <u>worn out</u> before I read all this information."

"<u>Calm down</u>. Let's <u>go over</u> this together. You can <u>get by</u> with just one very general book, if you find the right book," Brittany reassured me.

In the end it <u>did work out</u>. The librarian helped us <u>look for</u> a reference book which had a short paragraph about burial customs in almost every country.

Now, I know a lot about what is customary in different countries when someone <u>passes away</u>. All I have to do now is <u>take back</u> the books to the library.

1. die_____

2. postpone_____

3. be successful_____

4. meet accidentally_____

5. review_____

6. exhausted (tired)_____

7. visit (to a place)_____

8. return_____

9. assist_____

10. relax_____

11. succeed with a minimum effort_____

12. discover_____*find out*_____

13. search for_____

14. research_____

Exercise 2 *(Focus 2)*

Complete each sentence using a **phrasal verb** from the list on page 162 to describe the picture. The first one has been done for you as an example.

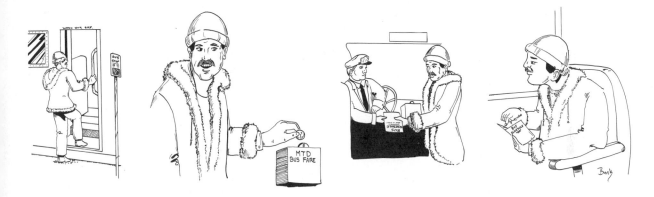

1. Patrick *gets on* a bus.

2. He _____ his ride.

3. He _____ a bus schedule.

4. He _____ his bus stop.

5. Louis _____ his girlfriend, Amy.

6. He _____ his best clothes.

7. He _____ Amy.

8. In a fancy restaurant, the waiter _____ them.

9. Angela _____ her apartment.

10. She _____ the trash.

11. Some friends _____.

12. She _____ the TV.

calls up	gets on	throws out
pays for	puts on	drop in
cleans up	turns off	picks up
waits on	picks up	looks for

Exercise 3 *(Focus 2)*

Some of the sentences from Exercise 2 have separatable verbs. Rewrite these sentences, separating the verbs.

E X A M P L E : *He picks a schedule up.*

1. _____

2. _____

3. _____

4. _____

5. _____

6. _____

7. _____

8. _____

Exercise 4 (Focus 3)

For each of the following **phrasal verbs**, write two sentences using the noun phrases at the right as cues. Separate the verb when possible.

E X A M P L E : pick up

        a package
        a package at the post office

Ann has to pick a package up.
She had to pick up a package at the post office.

turn off

        the radio
        all the electrical appliances before going
           on vacation

1. _____
2. _____

call up

        my mom and all my aunts and uncles
        my parents

3. _____
4. _____

throw out

        old papers
        the paper plates, cups, and decorations
           left over from the party

5. _____
6. _____

cheer up

        the sick and injured patients
        the patients

7. _____
8. _____

calm down

        the crowd of striking workers
        the children

9. _____
10. _____

| | put on | my sports coat, pants, and new dress shirt |
| | | my clothes |

11. _____

12. _____

| | look up | the number |
| | | the new address of the movie theater |

13. _____

14. _____

| | put off | my vacation |
| | | my trip to Japan, China, and Australia |

15. _____

16. _____

| | clean up | the wreckage from the airplane crash |
| | | our house |

17. _____

18. _____

UNIT 27

Participles as Adjectives

Exercise 1 (Focus 1)

Circle the correct adjective.

Sandy and Victor, both English teachers, lived abroad for many years, first in Saudi Arabia, and then in the Far East, where, like most travelers, they experienced culture shock. Recently they returned to the United States and experienced something that is called reverse culture shock. They had lived abroad for a very long time, and everything back home was new for them.

The cars seemed so big, and the people did too. They had forgotten how many overweight Americans there were. But everyone was obsessed / obsessing with dieting; they thought about it all the time. Every magazine seemed to have an article about dieting, but not many people seemed disciplined / disciplining enough to follow a diet. Most were disappointed / disappointing dieters.

When Sandy and Victor had first arrived in Saudi Arabia, it was surprised / surprising to see the Arab women covered / covering from head to toe. Sandy was equally shocked / shocking when she returned to the United States and saw women wearing rollers in public.

And both Sandy and Victor were frustrated / frustrating because they didn't have a car. When they lived abroad, transportation had never been a problem, but the North American city that they lived in had very poor public transportation; sometimes they had to wait an hour for the bus. It was very annoyed / annoying. And the bus stop was almost a mile from their apartment, so they had to walk a lot, too. At the end of the day, they were exhausted / exhausting.

It's difficult to return home after being in another country for a while. At first, Sandy and Victor were worried / worrying that they had a negative attitude about everything, but they felt relieved / relieving to hear about reverse culture shock. It will take time to feel comfortable living here again.

Exercise 2 *(Focus 1)*

Have you experienced culture shock? How about reverse culture shock? Write about your own experiences by completing the following sentences. Use the −*ed* or −*ing* form of the word in parentheses. If any of these adjectives don't reflect your own feelings or experiences, feel free to replace them with −*ed* or −*ing* forms that do.

1. I was (surprise) when I first saw

   _____

2. It was (frustrate) to

   _____

3. I was (confuse) when

   _____

4. It was (excite) to

   _____

5. I was (worry) that

   _____

6. It was (frighten) when

   _____

7. It was (fascinate) to see

   _____

8. I was (embarrass) when

   _____

9. I was (annoy) when

   _____

10. I felt (relieve) when

    _____

TOEFL® Test Preparation
Exercises · Units 25–27

Choose the <u>one</u> word or phrase that best completes the sentence.

1. Marcia gets _____ very early, before sunrise, so when she gets dressed, it's still dark.

   (A) off   (C) out

   (B) on   (D) up

2-3. This morning she must've been very _____ when she _____ her clothes.

   2. (A) tire   (C) tires

      (B) tired   (D) tiring

   3. (A) got dressed   (C) put on

      (B) got on   (D) took off

4. As usual, her friend _____ and they rode to work together.

   (A) picked her up   (C) ran into her

   (B) picked up her   (D) ran her over

5. Marcia was giving a presentation at work when she noticed that everyone looked very _____.

   (A) amuse   (C) amuses

   (B) amused   (D) amusing

6. Later on she _____ why everyone had been smiling during her presentation.

   (A) brought up   (C) went over

   (B) found out   (D) wore out

7. She had just finished talking on the phone, and as she _____, Marcia looked down at her feet.

   (A) held on   (C) hung up

   (B) hung on   (D) put down

8. She realized that she was wearing a blue shoe on her left foot and a brown shoe on her right foot; she had _____ the wrong shoes.

   (A) put away   (C) put off

   (B) put down   (D) put on

9. I don't think Marcia _____ crazy, do you?

   (A) doesn't go   (C) is going

   (B) goes   (D) isn't going

10. All of us have had _____ moments.

    (A) embarrassable   (C) embarrassful

    (B) embarrassed   (D) embarrassing

Identify the one underlined word or phrase that must be changed in order for the sentence to be grammatically correct.

11. I am convinced where New Orleans, Louisiana, with its Bourbon Street and its
     A   **B**   **C**
rhythmic jazz, is one of the most exciting cities in America.
                          D

12. Last fall I went over to my travel agency and asked my travel agent if she could find
            A   **B**
up about a trip to New Orleans during Mardi Gras for my sister and me.
 C   **D**

13. My sister's husband had passed away and I wanted to cheer up her by paying for a
              A   **B**   **C**   **D**
trip to New Orleans.

14. We were excited about the trip, but a little scared; once we were there, everything
     A   **B**
worked out, except my sister was shocking at what she saw on Bourbon Street.
    C   **D**

15. It was a fascinating trip—my sister ran to some old college friends, and we went out
       A   **B**   **C**
with them—so now she can't wait to go back for more ragtime jazz and Cajun food.
                  D

16. I am convince that our violent society is reflected by the increasing number of domes-
     A   **B**   **C**
tic-abuse cases that the police deal with, and the even higher number of abuses that
                  D
are not reported.

17. Every day women wake up to face another day of an abusing husband, and children
             A   **B**
watch with frightening faces—they know that they may be the next victim of their
     C   **D**
father's anger.

18. Abused women are frightened of their husbands and boyfriends, but they're even
 A   **B**
more afraid to report the abuse to the police because of what these abused men will
                               C
do to them after they find out.
             D

19. This violence is learned behavior: by example, parents teach their children that it's
       A   **B**
okay to hit someone when they're angry or frustrating—these children grow up and
                 C   **D**
act the same way to their children.

20. It is unlikely that this national problem won't end soon, but with education, a solu-
   A   **B**   **C**
tion will come about gradually.
        D

Conditional

Exercise 1 *(Focus 1)*

Three men have proposed to Eva. She doesn't know if she should marry Mack, Sato, or Travis. The following are predictions about her life. Make future conditional sentences using *if* and the verbs below.

E X A M P L E : marry Sato→ move to Tokyo

If she marries Sato, she'll move to Tokyo.

Sato—Japan

1. move to Tokyo→ have to learn Japanese

    _____

2. learn Japanese→ be the first one in her family to learn another language

    _____

Mack—hometown

3. marry Mack→ stay in Fremont, her hometown

    _____

4. live in Fremont→ not have to learn another language

    _____

5. not leave Fremont→ her life not change very much

    _____

Travis—$$

6. marry Travis→ be rich

    _____

7. live in a mansion→ feel like a princess

    _____

8. not feel like herself→ lose control over her life

    _____

9. marry Sato or Travis→ her life be more exciting

   _____

10. not get married→ not have to worry about this

   _____

Exercise 2 *(Focus 2)*

Make future conditional sentences by completing the following. Be careful with punctuation.

1. If the rain stops soon _____

2. My teacher will become angry if _____

3. If people stop fighting wars _____

4. I will say "You're welcome" if _____

5. If you go barefoot _____

6. I will leave the tip if _____

7. If you don't stop that _____

8. Oh, darling. If you leave me _____

9. If I never see you again _____

10. I'll be very happy if _____

Exercise 3 *(Focus 3)*

The following passage is about Constantine, a Romanian immigrant who lives in California and drives a taxi. Fill in the blanks with hypothetical conditionals. Be careful—some are negative.

1. If politics _____ (be) different, Constantine _____
   (have) to live in another country.

2. He _____ (live) in his apartment in Bucharest if he
   _____ (have) to live abroad.

3. He _____ (have) a decent life if he _____
   (live) in Bucharest.

4. If he _____ (know) more English, Constantine
   _____ (work) as an engineer; he _____
   (work) as a taxi driver.

5. His English is OK, but if he _____ (go) to school, he
   _____ (learn) more English, especially how to read and write.

170

6. Constantine _____ (live) in a nice apartment if he _____ (have) a decent job.

7. His life _____ (be) easier if he _____ (have) to wait for political asylum—it's been three years.

8. If he _____ (be) a resident, he _____ (bring) his family to the United States.

9. He _____ (be) happier if he _____ _____ (bring) his family to live here.

10. If Constantine's wife _____ (be) here, she _____ (have) to take care of the family alone.

Exercise 4 *(Focus 4)*

Put a check (✔) next to the sentences that are hypothetical (i.e., the situation probably won't happen).

1. __ I would move to Idaho if I won the lottery.
2. __ If I don't find a job here, I'm going to move to Idaho.
3. __ If Peggy were tall, she wouldn't have to look up at people.
4. __ Tom's going to marry Barb if he gets a promotion.
5. __ Tom would marry Barb if he made more money.
6. __ We wouldn't have these problems if we spoke Japanese.
7. __ If you go to Japan, you'll be able to practice your Japanese.
8. __ I won't go with you if you wear that outfit.
9. __ If they don't pay him more, he'll quit his job.
10. __ Bob would quit his job if the company transferred him.

Exercise 5 *(Focus 5)*

The following people are thinking about their past and how different individuals and events changed their lives. The pairs of sentences express what really happened in the past. Write hypothetical conditionals based on these sentences. The first sentence in the pair should be used in the *if* clause.

EXAMPLE: Mary went to the Bahamas on her vacation. That's where she met Gordon.
If Mary hadn't gone to the Bahamas, she wouldn't have met Gordon.

1. Mary met Gordon. That's why she didn't marry her high-school sweetheart.

   _____

2. Gordon went to medical school. Because of that, he didn't go to law school.

   _____

3. Gordon became a doctor. As a result, he didn't become a lawyer.

   _____

4. Claudia had Mr. Stack for algebra. Because of him, she passed math and she graduated from high school.

   _____

5. Mr. Stack was Claudia's teacher. As a result, she didn't quit school.

   _____

6. Barb married Tom. Because of him, she moved to Toronto.

   _____

7. Barb knew how to speak French and Spanish. That's why she got a job with an airline.

   _____

8. Jan got pneumonia. That's why she moved to Arizona.

   _____

9. Jan moved to Arizona. That's where she learned to ride a horse.

   _____

10. There wasn't birth control years ago. My grandmother had twelve children.

    _____

Exercise 6 (Focus 5)

Write hypothetical conditionals based on the following sentences. Be careful—some are in the present and some are in the past.

EXAMPLE: I didn't know that you needed me, so I went home.

If I had known that you needed me, I wouldn't have gone home.

1. I didn't give her the message because I didn't see her.

   _____

2. I won't be able to go with you this weekend because I don't have a bicycle.

   _____

3. I didn't know you were in the hospital, so I didn't visit you.

   _____

4. We got into trouble because we broke the law.

   _____

5. I didn't know we were going to be so late, so I didn't call you.

   _____

6. I ate the cookies because they were there.

   _____

7. You make mistakes because you're not careful.

   _____

8. Lexi isn't here, so we won't be able to solve this problem.

   _____

9. I don't have a car, so I take the subway.

   _____

10. You told me the news, so I knew.

    _____

Exercise 7 *(Focus 5)*

Complete the following conditional sentences. Be careful—not all of them are in the past.

1. I'd be a millionaire if _____

2. If I had more free time, _____

3. If I had been born a century ago, _____

   _____

4. I won't go if _____

5. If I were you, _____

6. He wouldn't have gone there if _____

   _____

7. She would buy that if _____

8. Their car wouldn't have been stolen if _____

   _____

9. If he had really loved her, _____

10. If my house were on fire, _____

11. If I could change one thing about my life, _____

_____

12. If he hadn't lost the contest, _____

13. If you had done what I told you to do, _____

_____

14. I'll go there with you if _____

15. I'd travel around the world if _____

_____

Question Review

Exercise 1 *(Focus 1)*

Complete the *yes/no* **questions** using the correct form of the word in parentheses. After the questions are completed, ask the questions to three of your classmates and record their answers on the chart. The first question has been formed for you.

Questions	Name: _____	Name: _____	Name: _____
1. _____*Can you*_____ swim? (can)			
2. _____ study on Saturdays? (do)			
3. _____ your mother live in the U.S.? (do)			
4. _____ be studying English next year? (will)			
5. _____ like to be a lawyer? (would)			
6. _____ English a difficult language for you? (be)			
7. _____ working now? (have)			
8. _____ ever _____ to Europe? (be)			
9. _____ watching TV last night? (be)			
10. _____ eat breakfast this morning? (do)			
11. _____ this activity fun? (be)			

Exercise 2 (Focus 1)

This is a yes/no question game. All students sit in a circle. One student begins by asking the student on his or her left a yes/no question. That student answers the question and then asks the student on his or her left another yes/no question, and so on around the circle. A student is "out" if: (1) she or he hesitates asking the question, (2) the question isn't formed correctly, or (3) she or he repeats a question that has already been asked. The game continues until only one student is left.

Exercise 3 (Focus 2)

Rewrite the questions in Exercise 1 as **statement form questions.** The first one has been done for you as an example.

1. *You can swim?*
2.
3.
4.
5.
6.
7.
8.
9.
10.
11.

Exercise 4 (Focus 2)

Read out loud each statement form question you wrote in Exercise 3. If possible, record yourself and listen to make sure you are using question intonation.

Exercise 5 (Focus 2)

Think of six things you would like to know about your classmates. Make a chart similar to the one in Exercise 1, but use your own questions. Make three of your questions **statement form questions,** and the other three *yes/no* **questions**.

Question	Name: _____	Name: _____	Name: _____
1. _____ _____			
2. _____ _____			
3. _____ _____			
4. _____ _____			
5. _____ _____			
6. _____ _____			

Exercise 6 *(Focus 3)*

Read the following questions and decide if the speaker expects the listener to answer *yes* or *no*. The first one has been done for you as an example.

	Yes	No
1. Isn't that Michael Jordan?	✔	—
2. Haven't you finished your homework yet?	—	—
3. Doesn't Rocio's apple pie look delicious?	—	—
4. Can't you do anything right?	—	—
5. Hasn't Marcia been to Disney World yet?	—	—
6. Are the trees beautiful in the fall?	—	—
7. Didn't you see that rock in the middle of the road?	—	—

Exercise 7 (Focus 3)

Complete the **negative questions** below.

1. Isn't _____

2. Don't _____

3. Doesn't _____

4. Won't _____

5. Couldn't _____

6. Weren't _____

Exercise 8 (Focus 3)

PAIR

Ask your partners five of the questions you wrote above. Write the answer you assume will be given and the actual answer that is given.

Question	Assumed Answer	Actual Answer
1. _____	_____	_____
2. _____	_____	_____
3. _____	_____	_____
4. _____	_____	_____
5. _____	_____	_____

Exercise 9 (Focus 4)

Verdieu Lucas is interviewing for a job as the director of the computer lab. Write the questions the interviewer is asking Verdieu. The first one has been done for you as an example.

Interviewer: *Which job are you applying for?*

Verdieu: I'm applying for the Lab Director's position.

Interviewer: _____

Verdieu: I think my strong points are that I know a lot about computers, that I get along well with otherpeople, and that I enjoy helping people use computers. Here's a copy of my resume.

Interviewer: _____

Verdieu: I'm looking for a full-time position. However, I'm willing to accept a part-time position to begin with.

Interviewer: _____

Verdieu: My native country is Haiti.

Interviewer: _____

Verdieu: I left my last job one month ago.

Interviewer: _____

Verdieu: I left that position because my family just moved here to Michigan.

Interviewer: _____

Verdieu: I know how to use both Apple and IBM computers, but I've had more experience with Apple.

Interviewer: _____

Verdieu: I will be available to work just about any time; however, I prefer to work during the day.

Interviewer: _____

Verdieu: I have missed only two days in the last two years because of illness.

Interviewer: _____

Verdieu: I have my own car, so getting to and from work isn't a problem.

Interviewer: _____

Verdieu: My references are my last supervisor and two of my instructors from when I was at the university.

Interviewer: _____

Verdieu: I can start working right away.

Interviewer: _____

Verdieu: I expect a fair salary for the work I do.

PAIR

Exercise 10 (Focus 4)

Choose one of the following jobs and role-play a job interview with a partner.

Waiter/waitress	Hotel desk clerk	Gas station attendant
Accountant	Teacher's aide	Singer in a night club
Medical receptionist	Mail carrier	Driver for a florist
Sales clerk in a department store		Carpenter

Exercise 11 (Focus 5)

Complete the following dialogues by adding the **tag questions** and completing the response. The first one has been done for you.

Catherine: You're taking a math class now, _____?

Jim: Yes, _____.

Catherine: Diana is in your class, _____?

Jim: Yes, _____.

Catherine: You both have to study a lot in calculus, _____?

Jim: Yes, _____.

Catherine: You'll finish the class soon, _____?

Jim: Yes,_____.

_____.

Catherine: Only three more weeks! Great. You're going to take a vacation after that, _____?

Jim: Yes, _____.

_____.

Catherine: Europe, that's great. You haven't been there before, _____?

Jim: No, _____

_____

Guillermo: You've been working here for a long time, _____?

Mary: Yes, _____. _____?

Guillermo: Twelve years! That is a long time. You were working here when Ms. O'Hara was the boss, _____?

Mary: Yes, _____.

Guillermo: You worked part-time at first, _____?

Mary: Yes, _____.

Guillermo: You don't get tired of all the typing and answering the phone, _____?

Mary: No, _____.

Guillermo: Yara's been here for a long time too, _____?

Mary: Yes, _____.

_____.

Guillermo: Longer than you! You both must really like working here,

_____?

Mary: Yes, _____.

Exercise 12 *(Focus 6)*

Read the dialogues in Exercise 10 with a partner. Read the first dialogue as though you are sure what your partner's answer will be. Read the second dialogue as though you are unsure. If possible, record yourself and listen to see if your intonation is falling or rising.

Emphatic Structures

Exercise 1 *(Focus 1)*

Read the following passage. Underline all the emphatic structures you can find. The first one has been done for you as an example.

Can you imagine a time when women had <u>no legal rights?</u> There was a time when women were considered part of their husbands' property. Married women had no legal existence and they could own no property. What was even worse was they could not keep any money they earned. It all went to their husbands. This really did seem unfair to many women.

Elizabeth Cady Stanton and Susan B. Anthony tried to change the unfair system. What they did was to write speeches and letters and hold conventions to organize women and men who supported legal rights for women. It was frustrating at first but they did finally win some small battles. In 1860, they worked to pass a law which did allow women to own property and control their wages in the state of New York. Other states soon followed.

But what many women really wanted was for women to be allowed to vote in elections. These women were called suffragettes. The suffragettes did win the right for women to vote in elections in some states. However, they weren't satisfied. What they fought for was a law that would allow women to vote in national elections. This change finally did happen in 1920. What happened was that the Nineteenth Amendment was passed. It finally gave women the right to vote in national elections.

Exercise 2 *(Focus 2)*

Match the phrases in part A with an appropriate word or phrase from part B. Connect them with an appropriate form of *be* and write the complete sentence in the space below. The first one has been done for you as an example.

A

1. What the problem was
2. What women were treated like
3. What married women couldn't do
4. What Susan B. Anthony and Elizabeth Cady Stanton did
5. What these women were called
6. What suffragettes wanted
7. What some states did
8. What finally happened

9. When it happened

10. What is happening today

B

women got the right to vote.

suffragettes.

equal rights and the right to vote.

property.

women had no legal rights.

own property or vote.

in 1920.

to write speeches and letters about women's right.

women are also becoming more equal in their wages.

pass state laws allowing women to vote.

1. *What the problem was was women had no legal rights.*
2. _____
3. _____
4. _____
5. _____
6. _____
7. _____
8. _____
9. _____
10. _____

Exercise 3 *(Focus 3)*

Agatha is trying to do her shopping, but she can't seem to find the right departments. Write what each sales clerk is saying under each picture. Be sure to use the emphatic forms. The first one has been done for you as an example.

Agatha: Where are the girdles?

Clerk: *What you need is the lingerie department.*

Agatha: I've got my girdle, now where are the hats?

Clerk: _____

_____

Agatha: This hat is perfect. Where can I find the toilet water?

Clerk: _____

_____

Agatha: A perfect scent, now what I need is support hose.

Clerk: _____

_____

Agatha: These are my size. Where can I get sandals?

Clerk: _____

_____

Joe is looking for a new car. Write what the salesman is saying under each picture. Be sure to use the emphatic forms.

Joe: I'm looking for something with good gas mileage.

Salesman: (1) _____

Joe: Well, I need a car.

Salesman: (2) _____

Joe: I need something that will hold all my skiing and diving equipment.

Salesman: (3) _____

Joe: I have to be able to carry at least 3 passengers.

Salesman: (4) _____

Joe: What I really need is a luxury car.

Salesman: (5) _____

Exercise 4 *(Focus 4)*

Work with a partner; take turns asking and answering the following questions using the appropriate emphatic verb form.

E X A M P L E : Do you like my new hat?

I certainly do like your new hat.

1. Did he win the lottery?_____
2. Have you tried Chinese food?_____
3. Will she make it to graduate school?_____
4. Does he exercise every day?_____
5. Are they happy living by themselves?_____
6. Can you find your way home?_____
7. Did you eat the whole meal?_____
8. Do you like my new car?_____
9. Is he coming home today?_____
10. Would you like some more spaghetti?_____
11. Is the food spicy enough?_____
12. Does it really taste like chocolate?_____
13. Have you been to Disney World?_____
14. Have you finished your finals?_____
15. Will you be here by 5:00?_____

Exercise 5 *(Focus 6)*

Read the following story. Then rewrite the story, replacing the underlined phrases with phrases using *no*. The first one has been done for you as an example.

Fractured Fairy Tale

Poor Cinderella was in a bad position. She had to work all day for her stepmother and ugly stepsisters <u>without a break.</u> She <u>didn't have time</u> to take care of herself, and <u>she didn't have any comforts.</u> She <u>didn't have a warm room, or a soft bed</u> to sleep in.

She could have run away from her mean stepmother and stepsisters, but then she would really have been in trouble because she would have been <u>without food, a home, money,</u> or <u>a job.</u> It seemed as though she <u>didn't have any way out.</u>

On the night of the royal ball, Cinderella was left by herself <u>without friends.</u> She <u>didn't have a dress or a ride</u> to the ball.

Suddenly, her fairy godmother appeared and told her not to worry because she could give her a dress.

Cinderella said, "No, thank you."

"What?" said her fairy godmother. "If you don't go to the ball, you won't meet your handsome prince and get married; you <u>won't have a husband.</u>"

"If it's OK with you, Fairy Godmother," said Cinderella, "<u>I don't want a husband.</u> I'd rather have a good education so I can get a better job."

The fairy godmother agreed with Cinderella and gave her the money to go to school instead of a dress.

Cinderella <u>isn't a princess</u> now; she's a lawyer fighting child abuse.

Poor Cinderella was in a bad position. She had to work all day for her stepmother and

ugly stepsisters with no break.

_____

_____

_____

_____

_____

_____

_____

_____

_____

_____

_____

_____

_____

_____

_____

_____

_____

_____

_____

_____

Exercise 6 *(Focus 7)*

Read the rewritten story of Cinderella orally. Emphasize all the negative aspects of the story. If possible, record yourself and listen to see how emphatic you sound.

Exercise 7 *(Focus 7)*

GROUP

Choose one of the following situations to role-play with your classmates. Emphasize all of the negative aspects of the situation.

1. You're on the first day of your vacation and you're disappointed with the hotel room because it is missing several things that you were promised by your travel agent. Complain to the hotel desk clerk. (Hint: Possibilities of things missing could be a view, hot water, towels, air conditioning or heating, water in the swimming pool, etc.)

2. You and your spouse both work, so you don't have much time to take care of the housework. One spouse complains about the condition of the house while the other complains about the lack of help he or she gets from the other spouse. (Hint: Possible complaints could be meals not cooked on time, laundry not done, shopping not done, etc.)

3. You have just taken a difficult test based on Unit 30 of your grammar book. You think the test wasn't fair because some of the things on the test weren't things that you studied in class. Complain to your teacher about the test.

Choose the <u>one</u> word or phrase that best completes the sentence.

1. _____ that an aluminum can? Yes, it is.
   - (A) Wasn't
   - (B) Isn't
   - (C) Aren't
   - (D) Weren't

2. Haven't you heard that can is recyclable? No, I _____.
   - (A) don't
   - (B) haven't
   - (C) didn't
   - (D) hadn't

3. _____ is some education about recycling.
   - (A) What do you need
   - (B) What you need
   - (C) You need
   - (D) What you needed

4. _____ do I need to know about recycling? Because it can make a difference.
   - (A) Where
   - (B) When
   - (C) Who
   - (D) Why

5. _____ that the resources of this planet are limited?
   - (A) Haven't you hear
   - (B) Didn't you heard
   - (C) Haven't you heard
   - (D) Did you heard

6. _____ mean? I mean that recycling aluminum saves energy because it takes less energy to recycle aluminum than to refine and produce new aluminum.
   - (A) What do you
   - (B) What you
   - (C) Do you
   - (D) Does he

7. Also, when people recycle, they reduce the amount of trash in landfills. If everyone recycled, we _____ have such a big problem with waste.
   - (A) will
   - (B) would
   - (C) won't
   - (D) wouldn't

8. There are other things besides aluminum that we can recycle, _____?
   - (A) are there
   - (B) aren't there
   - (C) is there
   - (D) isn't there

9. Sure, if you look in the phone book under recycling, you _____ a list of things that different companies recycle.

(A) will find
(B) would found
(C) are finding
(D) have found

10. _____ some of the things that can be recycled?

(A) Aren't
(B) How many
(C) What are
(D) Who are

11. You _____ newspapers, plastic bottles, cardboard, and glass, if you _____ each of them into different containers.

(A) can recycle . . . separate
(B) can recycle . . . would separate
(C) could recycle . . . will separate
(D) recycle . . . separated

12. All you have to do is separate your recyclables? That's easy, _____?

(A) hasn't it
(B) doesn't it
(C) isn't it
(D) didn't it

13. _____ recycling make sense?

(A) Aren't
(B) Isn't
(C) Wasn't
(D) Doesn't

14. I guess you're right. Recycling makes sense. I certainly _____ start recycling.

(A) am
(B) will
(C) was
(D) do

15. I'll get started right away. _____ put this can?

(A) Where should
(B) Where should I
(C) Where I should
(D) Should I

Identify the one underlined word or phrase that must be changed in order for the sentence to be grammatically correct.

16. Have you ever heard the story of the Cannibal Giant? No, I didn't.
     A   B   C   D

17. If you had lived many years ago, you might had met him. Who was the Cannibal Giant?
                                          A   B   C
What did he do?
     D

18. The cannibal giant was a monster. If he saw a child too far from his mother, the Cannibal
                            A   B
Giant would catch the child and eat him.
            C   D

19. He was terrible, <u>didn't he</u>? <u>Didn't</u> <u>anyone</u> <u>do</u> anything about the Cannibal Giant?
                      A   **B**   **C**   **D**

20. Yes, <u>what they did</u> is to make a trap. <u>What kind</u> of trap <u>did they</u> make? The men of the
           A **B**   **C**   **D**

   village dug a deep hole and covered it with branches.

21. Then <u>they</u> <u>asked</u>, "<u>How we can</u> <u>catch</u> the Cannibal Giant in the trap?
           A **B**   **C**   **D**

22. One brave little boy said, "If <u>I could</u> <u>get</u> the Cannibal Giant to chase me, I <u>would</u> <u>led</u>
                            A **B**   **C** **D**

   him to the trap."

23. The boy <u>really did</u> <u>got</u> the Cannibal Giant <u>to chase</u> him, and the Cannibal Giant
             A **B**   **C**

   <u>was caught</u> in the trap.
     D

24. However, the Cannibal Giant <u>was terrible</u>. He shouted at the people from the hole, "I
                               A

   <u>will</u> <u>no</u> die. I <u>will come</u> to drink your blood."
   B **C**   **D**

25. The people of the village <u>wanted</u> to make sure he <u>will</u> <u>no longer</u> be a problem; they
                       A   **B** **C**

   wanted <u>no more trouble</u> from the Cannibal Giant, so they threw burning logs into the
           D

   hole.

26. The Cannibal Giant shouted, "<u>You</u> think this <u>will finish</u> me? <u>If you don't</u> let me go, I
                         A   **B**   **C**

   <u>would come</u> to drink your blood."
     D

27. The villagers let the fire burn for three days, until the Cannibal Giant was <u>nothing</u> but
                                             A

   ashes. When the ashes <u>cooled</u>, they <u>stir</u> the ashes to see <u>if</u> the cannibal giant was still
                 B   **C**   **D**

   there.

28. <u>What happen</u> then? Millions of mosquitoes came out of the ashes. The mosquitoes
        A

   buzzed around the villagers and said, "<u>Did you think</u> you <u>could</u> destroy me? I <u>will come</u>
                               B   **C**   **D**

   to drink your blood."

29. If a mosquito <u>were</u> to talk to you today, you <u>would</u> <u>had heard</u> it saying the same thing.
   <u> </u>A   **B**   **C**   **D**